TAKING CHARGE

APR '98

TAKING CHARGE

TIME MANAGEMENT FOR PERSONAL & PROFESSIONAL PRODUCTIVITY

ERIC W. SKOPEC, PH.D. & LAREE KIELY, PH.D.

ADDISON-WESLEY PUBLISHING COMPANY, INC.
Reading, Massachusetts • Menlo Park, California • New York • Don Mills, Ontario
Wokingham, England • Amsterdam • Bonn • Paris • Milan • Madrid • Sydney
Singapore • Tokyo • Seoul • Taipei • Mexico City • San Juan

Many of the designations used by manufacturers and sellers to distinguish their products are claimed as trademarks. Where those designations appear in this book and Addison-Wesley was aware of a trademark claim, the designations have been printed in initial caps (i.e., Symphony).

The publisher offers discounts on this book when ordered in quantity for special sales. For more information please contact:

Corporate & Professional Publishing Group
Addison-Wesley Publishing Company
One Jacob Way
Reading, Massachusetts 01867

Library of Congress Cataloging-in-Publication Data

Skopec, Eric W., 1946-
   Taking charge : time management for personal & professional productivity /
Eric W. Skopec & Laree Kiely.
     p. cm.
   Includes bibliographical references and index.
   ISBN 0-201-55039-3 (pbk. : recycled and acid-free paper)
   1. Success—Psychological aspects. 2. Time management. 3. Time management—
Psychological aspects. 4. Goal (Psychology) I. Kiely, Laree. II. Title.
BF637.S8S55 1991
640'.43—dc20   91-4755
                         CIP

Cover design by Richard Rossiter
Text design by Wilson Graphics & Design (Kenneth J. Wilson)
Set in 10 point Palatino by Technologies 'N Typography

ISBN 0-201-55039-3

Contents

Preface

Getting ahead has never been easy. Today just keeping up is getting harder and harder. Without doubt, balancing busy personal and professional lives is a major challenge for many people.

If you've ever felt overwhelmed by your responsibilities, this book is for you. We've written it to help you dig out, clean your plate, and stay ahead of the game. We've gathered together many of the things you need to know to make your life more meaningful and rewarding as you cope with personal and professional responsibilities. In the following pages, you will learn how to:

- recognize subconscious patterns so you can take charge of your life,

- turn your dreams into reality by setting and achieving B.E.S.T. goals,

- organize your personal and professional life by taking advantage of powerful project management systems,

- handle interruptions and overcome procrastination,

- manage other people's time while turning losers into winners,

- stop wasting time in pointless, unproductive meetings, and

- make meaningful changes in your life and in the organizations around you.

Of course, none of this happens by itself—you've got some work to do. But we'll be right there with you, every step of the way, providing advice, encouragement, and the tools you need to get the job done.

In addition to the tools we provide, we'll also introduce you to some of the most important time management products on the market. You will find them described in sidebars—separate boxes like the one that follows.

> This is a sidebar. On the pages ahead, these boxes contain informative reviews of computer software and other products designed to help you manage your personal and professional life.

Today, you can choose from a seemingly endless supply of products to help you manage your time. They range from inexpensive desktop and pocket calendars to elaborate wall charts and notebooks. You can buy watches that store addresses and phone numbers while sounding alarms to remind you of appointments. Software developers offer programs that turn computers into personal assistants, and "palmtop" computers, the latest technological marvels, put the power of a computer in a package small enough to be carried in your purse or pocket.

While all of these products offer something of value, its often difficult to tell which ones will best suit your needs and interests, especially since new products appear overnight while old ones are revised or eliminated. We've done three things to help you make informed choices.

First, we have located reviews so you can consider the products in context. Rather than simply looking at a list of products, you will find them organized around the problems they solve. For example, project management software is reviewed in the chapter on organizing your life, financial management software in the chapter on setting and managing goals, and so forth.

Second, we have grouped products into general categories. For example, you will find notebook scheduling systems described in one sidebar, palmtop computers in another, project management programs in another, and so forth. In most cases we have reviewed only one or two of our favorite products in each category, but local retailers can direct you to other products of the same type if you want a broader selection.

Finally, we have tried to indicate the general usefulness of each product category. Our rating system differs a bit from those commonly used and we want to make sure you understand what our ratings indicate. All of the products described are good products—we wouldn't have listed them if they weren't. However, some satisfy a broader range of needs than others. Some provide functions not available elsewhere. Others merely add novel or interesting features to otherwise common products, or appeal to specialized, selected audiences.

Because we think of these products as productivity tools, we have used the following code:

🛠🛠🛠🛠 identifies a product that satisfies a need so fundamental that all professionals should use something of this type

🛠🛠🛠 designates an important product that satisfies a fundamental need but may duplicate something available less expensively through other means

🛠🛠 indicates an important product but for a more limited set of interests

🛠 points to a fun and interesting product, something that's nice to know about but doesn't fit the above categories

For example, we have rated notebook schedulers a 4 because we think everyone should use one. Computer based personal schedulers rate a 3 because they are important but paper-based systems will do many of the same things less expensively. We give automated time tracking and billing systems a 2 because they fill a real need for professionals who bill clients by the hour but are less generally needed. Business games rate a 1 because they are fun and useful but probably not essential.

All of the product descriptions are current at the time of writing. However you should be aware that new products are introduced every month, existing products are revised or withdrawn regularly, and manufacturers come and go with changes in the market. In general, these events work to everyone's advantage because product changes usually mean improvements. However, keeping up with the market can be a headache and we recommend you call the manufacturer (we've listed 800 phone numbers for many of them) or talk to a local retailer if you have difficulty finding any of the products we mention.

Introduction

HOP ON—WE HOPE YOU ENJOY YOUR RIDE WITH US!

Read the opening sentence a second or third time. It's an unusual way to start a book and we hope it will intrigue you.

The first sentence says a lot about our approach to time management, personal productivity, and our reasons for writing this book. As we look at things, each of us—readers and authors alike—is on a personal journey. Beginning the minute we are born and lasting at least until we take our final breath, we are moving through life at a pace we alone set or accept.

Think about your journey. As a child, you were wholly dependent on someone else. Every bit of food you ate was prepared by someone else. Everything you saw or did was controlled by someone else. Other people's perceptions were built into your view of the world. Much of your thinking was directed by the people around you.

As you matured, you began to exercise greater control over yourself and your environment. You began to realize that you had some impact on events and people. Think back to the first time you felt like you were in control of your own life, even for a moment. Maybe it was the first time your parents let you make an unescorted trip to a friend's home. Or maybe it was the first time your parents let you stay home alone while they went out for the evening. Whatever the experience was, it marked an important turning point in your life.

Over the years, more and more experiences contributed to the feeling of being "in charge." Recalling our own lives, we can add to the list of "firsts:" first car date, first vacation with friends, first apartment, and so forth. Your list may look a lot like ours. But even if the details differ the important point is the same: as you matured, you learned to control more of the things around you.

Your destination probably resembles ours: the feeling of independence that comes from having mastered some of the forces around us. This doesn't mean that we want to be isolated or to live our lives alone—far from it. It does mean that we want to be masters of our own fate—choosing where we live, with whom we spend time, what kinds of work we do, and how we make our mark on the world.

1

We think that our objective is shared by many people. And we know quite a few people who have been successful. They are happy with themselves and the people around them. Their lives are full and satisfying.

Unfortunately, we have also met quite a few people who have not been quite so successful. Some are just getting by. Others are angry and embittered. Family responsibilities, professional demands, even angry or oppressive bosses stand between them and their objectives. Although everyone's story is different, their disappointments seem to be tied up with their failure to take control of how they spend their time.

Look at that last sentence again. We're saying that success or failure is often tied to time management. That may be a startling statement. How can so much depend on something as simple as time management? The best answer we can give calls for a look at a few examples.

SOME NEW FRIENDS

Mary is an author and consultant. She has no family and few close friends, but no complaints. Her work fills her life and she often takes a portable computer with her on vacations. She is well paid, lives comfortably, and says her life is "like a dream come true." She works twelve hours a day, seven days a week, and seldom has fewer than six projects "in the works." She was writing two new books and splitting time between three major corporations when we last saw her.

John is a very successful executive with a major corporation. At thirty-seven, he is the youngest vice president in the history of the company and people in the know predict he will be the next president. His salary is well over $200,000 per year and he receives a generous bonus every year. In spite of his success, he frequently complains about his social life. "I just wish there was someone special in my life," he says. "I've got so much and it's really sad that there is no one to share it with."

Carl is a University professor with a distinguished research record. He has been an administrator and worked into a Dean's chair, which he resigned to get back to work on a book about eighteenth-century literature. His wife works as a secretary, but they barely make ends meet. Carl teaches half-time during the school year and devotes his summers to academic research. They seldom travel and never go first-class because it is far too expensive. Both Carl and his wife are bitter. "Society has no respect for real learning," they say. "Even minor league baseball players earn more than [Carl] does, and we just don't think it's fair."

KEEPING SCORE: WHAT IT MEANS TO BE A WINNER

Mary, John, and Carl are typical of the people we meet at our seminars and in our classes. As you read about them, you probably made some judgments about their lives. Even if you wouldn't trade places with her, you probably decided Mary was one of life's winners. She likes what she is doing and has no complaints.

You probably had mixed feelings reading John's story. He has been enormously successful in some respects but is beginning to feel that he has given up "too much." Work is his whole life. The fact that he is unhappy with his social life should come as no surprise—he devotes almost no time to social activities.

Finally, Carl and his wife look like losers. They are dissatisfied with their lives and they are bitter because, they complain, "society" has cheated them— they don't have enough money to live the way they would like. And their prospects of getting more money are not very bright. At best, they just hope to get along until they can retire.

THE MOST IMPORTANT PRINCIPLE

As you read about Mary, John, and Carl, we hope you can see the moral of the stories. Each has made choices about life and each is reaping the consequences of his or her choices.

Mary worked hard to get where she is. She has chosen an unconventional life-style and there was no one to show her the way. But she likes her life.

John and Carl have worked hard, too. The difference is that at least some of their effort has carried them in the wrong directions. John has begun to feel the need for more social contact and is beginning to make changes in the way he spends his time.

Carl has chosen to spend his time doing things that our society doesn't reward financially, at least not very well. He teaches half time and insists on having his summers free for research. Carl has chosen this life-style even though the study of eighteenth-century literature provides little compensation. The sad thing is that he and his wife are so bitter about the way "society" is treating them that they may never see that their own choices have created their lives.

PERSONAL CHOICES/PERSONAL HABITS

Mary, John, and Carl have all made choices about their lives, about how they spend their time. You may or may not approve of their choices, but the moral should be clear: the way you spend your time determines the kinds of rewards you get.

Mary and John are both conscious of the choices they have made. If you sit down to talk with her for a while, Mary will explain that she knew what she wanted to do by the time she was sixteen. She planned every step of her career and never feels the need to look back.

John planned every step of his career, too. The difference is that he doesn't like where some of the choices have taken him. Because he realizes that he made the choices, he knows that he can make different choices and has set out to "fix" his life. When he talks about his life, he openly explains that he always thought professional success was the most important thing. Now, he says, he realizes that other things are important, too, and he intends to make the changes needed to get them.

Carl is less willing to talk about his life, maybe because he doesn't like the way things have turned out. On the rare occasions when he opens up, it's clear that he isn't aware of the choices he's made. "I've always done what I was supposed to do," he says, "and I just don't think it's fair that I have so little."

Why is someone like Carl blind to the choices he has made? That is a tough question. Psychologists and other specialists could give you many answers. The one that makes most sense to us is that Carl made many choices so early in his life that he didn't realize he had any alternatives. He has always done what he was "supposed to do" and now those choices have become habits. Carl doesn't have to continue working on a book, but as long as he thinks that is what he is supposed to do, he may never consider the alternatives.

We agree that tenacity, simple stick-to-it-iveness, is an important trait. And we know that dozens of books on success have pointed out the necessity of perseverance. But we think it is time for Carl to reconsider his options. If he enjoyed his work enough to overcome his frustration, we wouldn't advise him to change. But, effective adults need to know when it's time to move on.

Even though Carl is an extreme case, all of us have made choices that we no longer think about. All of us have some habits that govern our lives, and all of us do what we're supposed to do. In this regard, Carl is no different than the company president who gets up at 5 A.M. every morning to read two or three newspapers and work out before going to work.

Habits aren't bad—in fact we probably couldn't get much done if we had to think about every move we make. But while habits make it possible for us to accomplish some things, they prevent us from accomplishing others.

The clock is running no matter what we do. Our habits determine when we start our day, how long it takes us to get to work, how much of ourselves we invest in our job, whom we socialize with, and when we go to bed at the end of the day. These habits form patterns that govern our lives with nearly predictable results.

We say "nearly predictable" because no one can deny the effects of luck. Carl's next book may be a runaway best seller. Or he may find a rare and valuable painting hidden in his attic. Or he may stumble upon a winning lottery ticket. Or . . . you get the point. A few people have extraordinarily good luck. And a few people have extraordinarily bad luck. But for most of us, luck is neutral and we get what we deserve—good, bad, or indifferent.

DISCOVERING YOUR OWN PATTERN

The patterns we see in people's lives are really approaches to time management. Without even thinking about it, you have been managing your time from the moment you began making decisions about your own life. You decided how much to work and how much to play. You decided how hard to work and how hard to play. And you decided how much time to devote to other activities.

We can't say that one pattern is better than any other. But we can say that different patterns are likely to produce different results. For example, people who spend all of their time at work are likely to accomplish more professionally than those who spend all their time watching television. Those who spend all their time sitting at a desk are likely to be less healthy than those who build regular exercise into their daily activities. And those who spend all their time in solitary activities are likely to have fewer friends than those who spend a lot of time in group activities.

The first step in making more of your life is discovering what patterns regulate your own life. The exercise on the next page is probably one of the most important things in this book and we encourage you to take it seriously. Understanding your own life pattern and what it's likely to produce is the starting point for developing a more satisfying, productive life. There is some background information we need to share with you at this point, but you may want to start observing your own pattern right now.

The First Step

Finding out what your patterns are is the first step to changing your habits. In fact, it's a good idea to take a systematic look at your time management habits even if you like most or all of the things that are happening in your life.

In our seminars, we use the example of a checkbook. What would you think of someone who never balanced his or her checkbook? Worse yet, what would you think of someone who didn't even keep track of the checks that had been written? We think failure to keep track of how you spend your time is a lot like failure to keep track of the checks you write.

The analogy between time and money is a pretty good one. More and more companies are starting to keep track of their professional employees' time—for good reason. The average salary for a manager in the United States edges toward $40 per hour *plus benefits* (an extra 30 percent in many organizations). From a personal point of view, keeping track of time is even more important—your whole life may hang in the balance.

On pages 8 and 9 is a form that you might use to keep track of your time. Feel free to make some copies for yourself if you would like to use it. You may also create your own form if you like, as long as it includes space to record time and activities.

Whether you use our form or one of your own, pick two or three days that you think are typical. A whole week might give you an even more accurate picture. Few people need to record seven full days: two weekdays and one weekend day is a convenient compromise. The days you pick are up to you, but remember your objective is to create a snapshot of your life. It's not a good idea to use vacation days or days at conferences or off-site meetings, unless you spend a lot of time in those activities.

On the days you choose, keep track of what you are doing in twenty-minute blocks. There is nothing magic about twenty-minute intervals. If you find yourself shifting frequently from one activity to another, you may prefer to use five or ten-minute blocks. On the other hand, you might use longer periods, thirty or sixty-minute chunks, if there are fewer changes in activity. The important thing is to make a relatively accurate record of your typical days.

One word of caution: don't take the exercise lightly. If you attempt to fill out the form at the end of the day you will get less out of the exercise than you deserve. Too many details will be forgotten by day's end, and the details you forget may hold the key to your growth. It is far more useful to keep your record as you go or to take a few minutes every hour to update the record.

The example on the pages 10 and 11 shows a form that has been filled out completely.

Budgeting Your Time

Just keeping track of your time is an important step toward increasing your personal productivity. By completing this step you have done something that few people—far too few, in our view—have ever done. The next step is even more important.

Step one was a lot like creating a checkbook register for your time. Step two is like creating a budget.

To begin creating your budget, go back to your time sheets and note how much time was spent on each activity. Then you need to begin looking at some general categories or patterns that describe your use of time. The following categories are a pretty good start.

(PM) personal maintenance: sleeping, eating, showering, shaving

(SD) self-development: exercise, professional reading, studying

($) financial: earning $, time on the job or in free-lance work

(SA) social activities: including time with family and friends

(CS) community service: voluntary work helping others, not for $

(RR) relaxation: resting, pleasure reading, sitting in the sun

(O) other

This set of categories is good enough for most purposes. There are a couple things you may want to keep in mind as you apply them.

First, some categories may overlap. For example, time spent watching TV with friends could be considered either social or relaxation time. The only important consideration is consistency. You can classify these activities in any way that makes sense to you as long as you do it consistently. You may need to create new categories to help you separate activities.

Second, some of the categories may not be sufficiently precise. For example, if you have several different projects at work, you might want to set up a separate category for each. Or if you have two or more jobs, you might want to have a category for each.

You can make the categories as precise as you like. Just don't make the categories so precise that you lose sight of the overall pattern. Don't let the trees keep you from seeing the forest.

The example on the pages 12 and 13 shows what your analysis might look like. Our form has a column for the analysis, but you can use a margin or piece of scrap paper if you prefer.

PERSONAL TIME RECORD

NAME _____   DATE _____

ACTIVITIES

Midnight

1:00 A.M

2:00 A.M.

3:00 A.M.

4:00 A.M.

5:00 A.M.

6:00 A.M.

6:20 A.M.

6:40 A.M.

7:00 A.M.

7:20 A.M.

7:40 A.M.

8:00 A.M.

8:20 A.M.

8:40 A.M.

9:00 A.M.

9:20 A.M.

9:40 A.M.

10:00 A.M.

10:20 A.M.

10:40 A.M.

11:00 A.M.

11:20 A.M.

11:40 A.M.

NOON

12:20 P.M.

12:40 P.M.

1:00 P.M.

1:20 P.M.

1:40 P.M.

2:00 P.M.

2:20 P.M.

2:40 P.M.

3:00 P.M.

3:20 P.M.

3:40 P.M.

4:00 P.M.

4:20 P.M.

4:40 P.M.

5:00 P.M.

5:20 P.M.

5:40 P.M.

6:00 P.M.

6:20 P.M.

6:40 P.M.

7:00 P.M.

7:20 P.M.

7:40 P.M.

8:00 P.M.

8:20 P.M.

8:40 P.M.

9:00 P.M.

9:20 P.M.

9:40 P.M.

10:00 P.M.

11:00 P.M.

MIDNIGHT

PERSONAL TIME RECORD

NAME _____ DATE _____

ACTIVITIES

Time	Activity
Midnight	sleep
1:00 A.M.	"
2:00 A.M.	"
3:00 A.M.	"
4:00 A.M.	"
5:00 A.M.	"
6:00 A.M.	morning jog
6:20 A.M.	"
6:40 A.M.	"
7:00 A.M.	shower/shave
7:20 A.M.	breakfast/read newspaper
7:40 A.M.	"
8:00 A.M.	drive to office
8:20 A.M.	"
8:40 A.M.	read morning mail
9:00 A.M.	return phone calls
9:20 A.M.	"
9:40 A.M.	review current status reports
10:00 A.M.	"
10:20 A.M.	"
10:40 A.M.	prepare for staff meeting
11:00 A.M.	staff meeting
11:20 A.M.	"
11:40 A.M.	"

NOON	lunch with vendor representatives
12:20 P.M.	"
12:40 P.M.	"
1:00 P.M.	"
1:20 P.M.	"
1:40 P.M.	return phone calls
2:00 P.M.	read quarterly reports
2:20 P.M.	"
2:40 P.M.	"
3:00 P.M.	plant walk through
3:20 P.M.	"
3:40 P.M.	"
4:00 P.M.	"
4:20 P.M.	read quarterly reports
4:40 P.M.	"
5:00 P.M.	"
5:20 P.M.	pick up son at baseball practice
5:40 P.M.	drive home
6:00 P.M.	help prepare dinner
6:20 P.M.	dinner with family
6:40 P.M.	"
7:00 P.M.	"
7:20 P.M.	help clear table
7:40 P.M.	watch TV with family
8:00 P.M.	"
8:20 P.M.	"
8:40 P.M.	"
9:00 P.M.	read professional journals
9:20 P.M.	"
9:40 P.M.	"
10:00 P.M.	late news on TV
11:00 P.M.	to bed

PERSONAL TIME RECORD

NAME _____   DATE _____

ACTIVITIES

PM	Midnight	sleep
PM	1:00 A.M.	"
PM	2:00 A.M.	"
PM	3:00 A.M.	"
PM	4:00 A.M.	"
PM	5:00 A.M.	"
PM	6:00 A.M.	morning jog
PM	6:20 A.M.	"
PM	6:40 A.M.	"
PM	7:00 A.M.	shower/shave
PM	7:20 A.M.	breakfast/read newspaper
PM	7:40 A.M.	"
$	8:00 A.M.	drive to office
$	8:20 A.M.	"
$	8:40 A.M.	read morning mail
$	9:00 A.M.	return phone calls
$	9:20 A.M.	"
$	9:40 A.M.	review current status reports
$	10:00 A.M.	"
$	10:20 A.M.	"
$	10:40 A.M.	prepare for staff meeting
$	11:00 A.M.	staff meeting
$	11:20 A.M.	"
$	11:40 A.M.	"

$	NOON	lunch with vendor representatives
$	12:20 P.M.	"
$	12:40 P.M.	"
$	1:00 P.M.	"
$	1:20 P.M.	"
$	1:40 P.M.	return phone calls
$	2:00 P.M.	read quarterly reports
$	2:20 P.M.	"
$	2:40 P.M.	"
$	3:00 P.M.	plant walk through
$	3:20 P.M.	"
$	3:40 P.M.	"
$	4:00 P.M.	"
$	4:20 P.M.	read quarterly reports
$	4:40 P.M.	"
$	5:00 P.M.	"
SA	5:20 P.M.	pick up son at baseball practice
SA	5:40 P.M.	drive home
SA	6:00 P.M.	help prepare dinner
SA	6:20 P.M.	dinner with family
SA	6:40 P.M.	"
SA	7:00 P.M.	"
SA	7:20 P.M.	help clear table
SA	7:40 P.M.	watch TV with family
SA	8:00 P.M.	"
SA	8:20 P.M.	"
SA	8:40 P.M.	"
SD	9:00 P.M.	read professional journals
SD	9:20 P.M.	"
SD	9:40 P.M.	"
RR	10:00 P.M.	late news on TV
PM	11:00 P.M.	to bed

Checking Your Balance

The final step is summarizing what you've discovered. You could list by hours and minutes but we find it easier to do everything by minutes so you don't have to convert figures later.

	Day 1	*Day 2*	*Day 3*
personal maintenance:	540 min	520 min	620 min
self-development:	60 min	60 min	150 min
financial:	560 min	540 min	50 min
social activities:	220 min	180 min	440 min
community service:	0 min	0 min	0 min
relaxation:	60 min	140 min	180 min
other:			

Just looking at the total number of minutes in each category should give you much of the information you need. Occasionally you get a better perspective by converting the numbers to percentages. Just divide the raw numbers by 1440, the number of minutes in each day.

personal maintenance	37.5%	36.1%	43.1%
self-development:	4.2%	4.2%	10.4%
financial:	38.8%	37.5%	3.5%
social activities:	15.3%	12.5%	30.5%
community service:	0%	0%	0%
relaxation:	4.2%	9.7%	12.5%
other:			

You can even take the analysis one step further by converting your percentages into a pattern for a whole week. Because we chose two weekdays and one weekend day, you can convert to a comprehensive picture by multiplying percentages for each weekday by 2.5, multiplying percentages for the weekend day by 2, adding numbers in each category, and dividing by 7. The numbers from our example give the following pattern.

personal maintenance	38.7%
self-development:	6.0%
financial:	28.3%
social activities:	18.5%
community service:	0%
relaxation:	8.5%
other:	

This analysis shows what your habits are. We wouldn't say that any distribution is right or wrong. However, you need to decide whether or not you are happy with what you find. If you don't like what you see, you can make changes using the powerful goal setting procedures introduced in the next chapter.

ANOTHER BOOK ABOUT TIME MANAGEMENT

Even though you've come this far with us, you may be wondering why we've written another book about time management. After all, time management is probably one of the most popular topics of the last two or three decades. The shelves of most major book stores have at least a half dozen books on the subject. Some of the better ones include Alan Lakein, *How to Get Control of Your Time and Your Life;* Michael LeBoeuf, *Working Smarter;* R. Alec Mackenzie, *The Time Trap;* Beverly Benz Treuille and Susan Schiffer Stautberg, *Managing It All;* and Stephanie Winston, *The Organized Executive.* These are all good books and everybody can learn something from them.

With so many books on time management, do we really need another one? We think so, and the fact that you are looking at this introduction suggests that you think so, too. Let us tell you why we chose to write another book on such a popular topic.

First, although there are several good books on time management, we think we have an important contribution to make. Many of the other books focus on a specific aspect of time management. For example, some deal with setting priorities. Others focus on "tricks of the trade" and still others concentrate on "getting organized." These are all important topics and no book on the subject would be complete if it didn't at least mention them. Where we differ from some others is that we think setting priorities, mastering tricks of the trade, and getting organized are important because they help you become more productive. Our focus on productivity is distinctive. We think that there is a great deal to be said about productivity, no matter what you do for a living or what you would like to accomplish with your life.

Our second reason for writing this book is related to the first. Many of the books that are already "out there" make it seem that the only important things in their readers' lives happen at work. In fact, many of the books seem to focus upon helping you to get more done for somebody else: your boss, the company president, the stockholders, or—if you are employed by a governmental agency— the public. Don't get us wrong! We think it is important to get things done for other people, your boss, the company president, the stockholders, or the public. After all, that is often the best way to get ahead.

But isn't there more to your life? Aren't there things in your life you want to accomplish for yourself or your family? Things that have nothing to do with your job, your boss, the company president, the stockholders, or the public? Personally, we found that there are many things in our lives that have nothing to do with our jobs but are still important. As we tried to achieve balance in our lives we were drawn to readings and personal philosophies that had a lot to say about how we should use our time, but were never even mentioned in the popular time management books. The more we read, the more certain we became that a complete book about time management ought to touch on these seldom mentioned issues. Futhermore, we think that the same time management tools you use at work should be useful in your daily lives as well.

Finally, many of the popular books simply fail to take account of some of the technological changes taking place around us. Cellular phones, facsimile machines, and personal computers have all burst on the scene since the classic time management books were written. Today, you don't need to be a "techie" to take advantage of these marvels. In fact, we wonder how professionals who don't take advantage of them survive. A quick example will show you what we mean.

One of the authors used to be incurably messy. A brief look into his office would send many people into convulsive laughter. Scraps of paper covered the desk, boxes of note cards and stacks of business cards covered the desk calendar, while a rolodex, portable typewriter and alarm clock teetered precariously atop a pile of telephone books.

Today, much of the clutter is gone. A single program, *Windows 3.0*, has moved the odds and ends out of sight, into a personal computer. An electronic clock built into *Windows 3.0* keeps track of time while the Calendar program organizes appointments and even sounds an alarm when it is time to go. Note cards, business cards, the rolodex, and even scraps of paper have been replaced by the NOTE CARD feature while paper, pens, and the portable typewriter have given way to the text editor, a program called WRITE. And, when it's time for a break, a click on the mouse brings up an entertaining game of solitaire or REVERSI.

Windows 3.0 runs on IBM AT and fully compatible computers with 1 megabyte RAM and an Intel 286, 386, or 486 central processing unit.

Older personal computers including original IBM PC and XT computers, and many inexpensive clones are not powerful enough to run *Windows 3.0*. Fortunately a new program, *Ensemble* makes many features of *Windows 3.0* available to owners of less powerful computers.

Ensemble, like *Windows*, is a graphical user interface which means that you start programs by using a mouse to "click" on pictures associated with them rather than by entering typed commands. Both *Windows* and *Ensemble* make it possible to run several programs at once in separate windows and both manage larger amounts of computer memory than the disk operating system (DOS) supplied with most computers. Like *Windows 3.0*, *Ensemble* provides several applications programs for writing, drawing, filing, and scheduling.

Windows 3.0 is currently available from Microsoft; One Microsoft Way; Redmond, WA 98052-6399; (800) 323-3577 or (206) 882-8088; for $99. It is frequently packaged with new computer systems.

Ensemble runs on IBM PC and fully compatible computers with a hard disk, graphic display, and at least 512K RAM. It is currently available from GeoWorks; 2150 Shattuck Ave; Berkeley, CA 94704; (415) 664-0883; for $195.

While the immediate availability of powerful computers allows us to use programs like *Windows*, it has also increased the pressures under which we work. Answers that used to be good enough—we called them "approximations"—just don't cut it any more. When we begin to use computers to produce more precise answers we find that even minor errors can be multiplied by unseen forces. A misplaced decimal point in one cell of a spreadsheet can make a difference of millions of dollars in the total. And even if we chose not to use a computer, keeping up with coworkers and competitors who use them can become a full-time job.

To the best of our knowledge, this is the first book on personal productivity to include a somewhat systematic reference to some of the technology that may shape our personal lives. Throughout this book, you will find references to products and services that make it easier to manage our lives productively.

As people have gotten used to working on PCs, there has been a growing demand for computers that can travel with their owners. The first portable computers were really "lugable" machines. They weighed twenty or more pounds and barely fit under airplane seats.

Laptop computers were introduced next and remain popular because they pack a lot of power in relatively small containers. Today, you can easily buy a laptop computer weighing less than ten pounds which is nearly as powerful as the one on your desk. Laptop computers may include relatively fast processors, hard disks, and battery packs supporting three or four hours of working time.

Although today's laptop computers are extremely powerful, most are still too large to classify as personal assistants. Palmtop computers, the next generation, are intended to put the power of computing in your pocket.

The first palmtop computers on the market forced users to make quite a few compromises. Laughably small screens, unusual keyboard arrangements, and limited ability to exchange information with other computers were just some of the annoyances. However there are now several palmtops worthly of serious consideration.

Our favorite palmtop under $500 is the *Atari Portfolio*. This compact wonder puts an awful lot of power in a package weighing under 1 pound. Measuring just 7.8 × 4.1 × 1.2 inches, *Portfolio* features built-in applications including DOS 2.11, a spreadsheet, word processor, telephone/address book, appointment diary with multiple alarms, and a calculator. New software includes a file manager and financial analysis routines.

Powered by three AA batteries, *Portfolio* features a standard 63-key QWERTY keyboard and eight-line screen which serves as a window on an 80 × 25 character display. Options include interfaces for transferring information back and forth to a full-sized PC, additional RAM memory cards, and an AC adapter.

The *POQET* computer stands out in the over $500 category—and we mean well over $500. *POQET* is about the same size and weight as *Portfolio*, but is as close to state of the art as any commercial product we have seen. It has an 80 × 25 character screen, standard QWERTY keyboard with 77 keys including 12 function keys, and an embedded numeric keypad. Built-in read-only memory includes DOS 3.3, GW Basic, and five applications programs: PoqetCalc, a standard four-function calculator; PoqetWrite, a screen editor for writing and editing notes or memos; Poqet-

Schedule, a calendar with appointment scheduler, alarm, and to-do list; Poqet-Address, an address book; and PoqetTalk, an easy-to-use communications program that allows you to use a modem or connect the Poqet to another computer.

In addition to its built-in software, *Poqet* has two "drives" for memory cards. These cards provide increased storage space—up to 512 K each—and may be used to load additional programs including AlphaWorks. AlphaWorks provides a word processor with spelling checker and thesaurus, a database manager, a spreadsheet, and a communications program. AlphaWorks files are compatible with those used by several more common programs so it is easy to share information with other computer users.

The recently released *HP 95LX* fills an important price niche between the *Portfolio* and *Poquet*. Measuring 1 by 3.5 by 6.25 inches, the *HP 95LX* weighs 11 ounces and has an 80-key QWERTY keyboard with separate function keys and numeric keypad. The relatively easy-to-read screen displays 40 columns by 16 rows. Built-in software includes MS-DOS 3.22, Lotus 1-2-3, and the Appointment Book, Phone Book, Memo Editor, Financial Calculator, Filer, and Data Communication Utility. Options include RAM cards up to 512 K, an AC adapter to extend life of the two AA batteries, and a "Connectivity Pack" for transferring files to desktop computers.

Portfolio and *Poqet* put considerable power in tiny packages. However both are characterized by very small keyboards. Neither of them, nor their competitors, facilitate touch typing.

Portfolio is currently available from Atari Corporation; Post Office Box 61657; Sunnyvale, CA 94088; (800) 443-8020; for $399.90 for a base unit. *Poqet* is produced by Poqet Computer Corporation; 650 N. Mary Avenue; Sunnyvale, CA 94086; (800) 624-8999; for $1450 and up. The *HP 95LX* is manufactured by Hewlett-Packard Company; 1000 NE Circle Boulevard; Corvallis, Oregon 97330; (800)443-1254; for a suggested retail price of $699.

WHAT LIES AHEAD

This introduction has explained our philosophy and pointed you in the direction of increased personal productivity. We hope you enjoy the rest of the journey.

The next stop, chapter 1, will help you identify things that are really important to you. We call them "differences that make a difference," and identifying them is the foundation for a powerful goal-setting process that will help you make changes in the habits you've identified.

Chapter 2 introduces a project-centered approach to organizing your life. It will show you how to pursue the goals set in Chapter One and how to keep track of your progress.

Chapter 3 introduces some "tricks of the trade" that will help you cope with interruptions, while Chapter 4 shows how to make more effective use of others' time.

Chapter 5 tackles one of the most frustrating time wasters—meetings. The Conclusion outlines a step-by-step procedure to apply what you have learned to your whole life.

There is one thing we'd like you to keep in mind on your journey: success, however you define it, doesn't necessarily mean working harder. Doing the right things, working smarter, is at least as important as the amount of effort you invest. Good luck on the rest of your journey. Please stop back and see us whenever you feel the need.

SUGGESTED READINGS

Douglass, Merrill E., and Donna N. Douglass. *Manage Your Time, Manage Your Work, Manage Yourself.* New York: AMACOM, 1980.

Lakein, Alan. *How to Get Control of Your Time and Your Life.* New York: Peter H. Wyden, Inc., 1973

LeBoeuf, Michael. *Working Smarter.* New York: McGraw-Hill Book Company, 1979.

Lee, Mary Dean. "The Great Balancing Act: Unseen Ways of Structuring Our Lives Can Tip the Scales Between Frustration and Fulfillment." *Psychology Today,* March 1986, 48–54.

Mackenzie, R. Alec. *The Time Trap.* New York: AMACOM, 1972.

Rehnquist, William H. "Time; It's Yours to Use or Abuse." *Vital Speeches,* 1 July 1987, 549–51.

Treuille, Beverly Benz, and Susan Schiffer Stautberg, *Managing It All.* New York: Master Media, 1988.

Webber, Ross A. *Time Is Money!* New York: The Free Press, 1980.

Winston, Stephanie. *The Organized Executive.* New York: W. W. Norton & Company, Inc., 1983.

Chapter 1

GOAL SETTING

CRITICAL SUCCESS FACTORS
AT HOME AND AT WORK

The way we spend our time determines the results we get, but there is a complication: there are different kinds of time. Some of our time is controlled by other people, some time is managed by the systems in which we participate, and some time is ours alone to control. Let's take a minute to look at a day in the life of a typical manager.

A TYPICAL DAY

Marilyn Smith is a relatively new production manager for a consumer products company. Marilyn is 32 with twin boys in school and a working husband, Brad. Marilyn's time is carefully budgeted and she gets a lot done in a typical day.

Marilyn gets up at 6:00 every morning. She packs lunches for the boys, gets their clothes ready for school, and makes breakfast while Brad is showering and shaving. Marilyn wakes the children at 7:00 and gets ready for work while they dress and eat breakfast. By 7:45 she is ready to go and has a moment to grab a quick breakfast for herself before packing the children into her car.

Marilyn drops the children at their school on her way to work. A bus will take them to a day care center at the end of the school day and she will pick them up on her way home in the evening.

As usual, Marilyn gets to her office by 8:30. She starts her day in the office with a cup of coffee while reviewing mail and production reports from the previous day. She also takes time to return any phone calls that she didn't have time for the day before. She meets with her first line supervisors briefly at 10 every day and walks the shop floor—"just to say hello to everyone," she says—on her way to the daily staff review meeting with her boss at 11:00.

Marilyn takes an hour lunch at noon, but it is seldom restful. Today she needs to get some things for her children's school projects and she stops to pick up some clothes at the laundry on her way back to work. Lunch consists of a hamburger and some greasy fries from a fast food stand along her route.

Getting back to the office at 1:15—"late again" she reprimands herself—Marilyn walks through the plant again, stopping to talk with anyone who wants to chat. There are a half dozen phone messages waiting for her when she gets to her office. One or two can wait, but several need answers and she finally finishes returning calls by 2:45.

"At last," she says, "I have some time to work on the production report." She pulls three large files from her desk drawer and begins sorting their contents. Her boss has asked her to review recent production figures and account for some periods of unusually low output. He made the request almost six weeks ago, but there just hasn't been enough time. Now he is getting anxious and his requests have gotten unusually pointed.

"It's about time I got this off my back," she said to herself, just as there is a knock on her door. John, one of her first line supervisors, wants to see her about a personal problem. "It will only take a minute" he says. The look on his face is enough to tell Marilyn that she better take some time with him so she breaks for a cup of coffee while they talk.

John's concerns turn out to be relatively minor, and he was relieved to have a chance to talk to her. Marilyn finally gets back to work on her report at 4:15. She is starting to feel guilty about the report and doesn't really care to get more static from her boss, so she asks her secretary to hold her calls and screen visitors. The tactic works—this time at least—and she gets to concentrate long enough to write out a rough draft of the report. But it is almost 6:15 when she finishes and she realizes that she will probably be late picking up her children.

Tossing the report in her briefcase, Marilyn grabs her coat and races to her car. Taking shortcuts through mall parking lots and running a couple of red—"almost yellow" is her phrase—lights, she manages to get to the day care center by 6:35. "Only five minutes late," she congratulates herself.

Both boys are tired and hungry, and they are beginning to whine by the time she gets home. Brad has a pleasant surprise waiting when they arrive: he realized they were running late and he has dinner on the table as they come in the front door. After dinner, Marilyn clears the table and gets the dishes into the washer while Brad gets the boys ready for bed. They are asleep by 8:30, and Marilyn takes an hour to watch TV, relax, and talk to Brad.

At 9:30 she slips off to the dining room to work on her report. It still isn't finished by 10:45, but she is too tired to do any more. Brad is already asleep when she gets to bed, so she curls up next to him and falls asleep thinking about what she needs to do the next day.

This was a fairly typical weekday for Marilyn. Her weekends follow a different schedule but that doesn't necessarily mean that she has much free time. She seldom goes to the office, but she likes to catch up on housework, do grocery and other shopping, spend some time with her children, and get in an occasional workout.

As you can see, Marilyn's time is carefully budgeted. Her days are full and they may even be like many of yours: long, active, and tiring. You could also say Marilyn's time is well spent and her days are productive because she gets a lot done. But you might wonder if she is really happy keeping such a tight schedule. You may also notice that she doesn't really control all of her time. Let's take a closer look at how she spent her typical day.

Like most of us, Marilyn spends about one third of her day at work. If you look closely, you can see that she spends her time on three different kinds of activities.

First, she spends some time doing things that her boss tells her to do. The time she spent working on the production report is a good example. Virtually all of us spend some of our time at work responding to requests from our superiors.

Second, Marilyn spends some time doing things that the system requires her to do. These are tasks that she has to do because she is a manager. Returning work-related phone calls is a good example. Attending meetings is another good example.

Finally, Marilyn spends some time doing things that she decides need to be done. Walking the floor to talk to employees and taking time to discuss a personal problem with the supervisor are good examples.

These three kinds of time make up the days of most professionals. How much time someone spends on each says a lot about their position in an organization. In general, lower level employees spend most of their time on tasks assigned by their supervisors. More experienced, mature, or trustworthy employees spend more time responding to system-imposed demands. Relatively senior employees are expected to show more initiative and spend more time on self-imposed activities.

If we look at how Marilyn spends her time away from work, we see a similar pattern. She doesn't really have a "boss," but she does spend a lot of time doing things for other people. For example, she packs lunch for her children and even runs errands for them on her lunch hour.

Marilyn also spends some time doing things required by "the system." Of course the system isn't as clearly defined at home as it is at work, but there are some things that she must do as a result of her position in the family. Driving the boys to school and picking them up in the evening are good examples of system-imposed time. The biggest difference between system-imposed time at home and at work is that Marilyn might have an easier time changing the system at home than at work. But even there, any alterations in her system-imposed time would probably require her husband's cooperation.

Finally, Marilyn also had a little self-imposed time at home. There wasn't very much today, but watching television in the evening is an example.

Even if you aren't married, don't have any children, or don't have a job, you have something in common with Marilyn and with every other reader of this book: your day consists of boss-imposed, system-imposed, and self-imposed time. Like it or not, your day is spent doing things for other people, doing things for a system, or doing things for yourself.

You also need to ask yourself a couple of questions which may have already occurred to you while reading about Marilyn's day: Is she spending her time wisely? Is she really happy living that kind of schedule? It is easy to ask those questions about someone else, but it may be harder to ask them of yourself. Let's try a brief experiment before we look for a personal answer.

THE DREAM VACATION

Set aside some time for this exercise; pick a time and place where you won't be interrupted for at least an hour. You will need a few pieces of writing paper and a pen or pencil. Don't rush! Take enough time to work out your answers with care.

Imagine that you are sitting at home one evening when there is a knock at the door. As you open it you are greeted by a well-dressed gentleman. He introduces himself as Mr. Johnson and asks to come in to talk to you "about a matter of great importance." You let him in and sit down to talk in your living room.

Mr. Johnson explains that you have been awarded an unusual prize with very few restrictions. The prize is an all expense paid vacation. For two months, all of the things that worry you will be taken care of. You will have all the money you need, your family and friends will be cared for. Your job will be put "on hold" so you can come back and pick up right where you left off. And you have unlimited money for two months. That's right, you can buy absolutely anything you want; the money will never run out.

There are a few restrictions: at the end of two months, anything that is left over must be returned to the company that awarded you the vacation. Cars, houses, furniture, savings bonds, bank deposits, airline tickets, food and liquor, in short, everything that is left must be returned. You won't be billed for the things you used, but you can't keep anything that you purchased.

Now here is the tough question: What would you do on your two-month vacation from worry? Where would you go? Who would you see? What would you buy? How would you spend your time?

Be inventive in your answer. Try to list everything that you would do for the two months. Let your dreams be your guide; don't leave anything out. Use paper and pencil to make notes for yourself if you like, but this is a private exercise and you don't need to share your results with anyone else.

If you have time now, set this book aside and pick it up again when you have finished. If you don't have time now, mark this page and come back to the exercise later. We think you will see that the time is well spent.

We call this exercise creative day dreaming. True, it isn't very "realistic"—it isn't supposed to be. We have a very good reason for making it unrealistic. All too often the things we call "realistic" are really limitations imposed by our experiences and habits. They are like the system-imposed expectations that shape our lives without our consent. They are the things we are "supposed to do" or "ought to do" without ever knowing why. But once we get away from them, once we take a moment to dream, it is easier to see what really matters to us.

Let's take a look at some relatively impersonal parts of Marilyn's list. The list says a lot about her and we may learn something about ourselves by looking at her example.

Marilyn's Dream Vacation

1 week by myself; just me alone on a deserted island. Brad and the kids can fend for themselves while I get back in touch with myself.

3 weeks to travel; Brad and I will take the kids to all the places we wanted to go ourselves but could never afford.

3 weeks back in our home town; we'll visit friends and relatives we haven't seen for ages, especially our friends from college.

1 week back to work but with a few changes; I'll be the boss and show people how things should be done. No more last minute changes in orders. No more blaming people on the floor for management's errors. No more 14 hour days without pay—everybody will work a 6 hour day so they will have time for home, family, and personal growth.

Marilyn's list says a lot about her. You might want to ask whether she is really happy with her go-go schedule? Does she like to put in all that time at work? Do material things matter much to her? How much of her fantasy has to do with things she might like to buy (a new house, car, mink coat)? And how does the time in her dream vacation compare to her current schedule?

You may see other things in Marilyn's list that you want to discuss. If you do, pick a friend or colleague that you trust and ask him or her them to go over the list with you. Once you think you have gotten everything out of Marilyn's list that you can, go back and look at your own list. What does it say about you? Would you like to travel? Have more time for leisure? Get a promotion at work? Own your own company? Buy things for yourself, family, friends?

There are no right or wrong answers to this exercise. The important thing is to begin forming a sense of what really matters to you. For some people, it will be time with family and friends. Other people will want to get ahead at work or own their own companies. Many people would like to travel and some would like a new home or car, even for only two months. As long as you were honest, your answers can provide important directions.

Don't be afraid to come back and try this experiment again in a few months. People change and so do their wants. We know some very successful people who come back to this exercise every six months just to be sure they are still on the "right track."

Creative dreaming can help you identify what you really want to do. And comparing your dream to the way you actually spend your time is a convenient measure of how well you are doing. What do you do if you don't like what you find? How do you turn your dreams into reality? Which of your "someday I'm gonnas" are you willing to turn into "I wish I hads?" Goal setting is the answer to these questions.

TURNING DREAMS INTO REALITY

Countless success stories are told about people who have used goal setting procedures to turn their dreams into reality. There is no doubt that setting goals and striving to accomplish them is an important technique in increasing personal productivity. In a minute we will talk about some specific features of goals that promote high levels of performance. But first we will consider why goal setting has such a powerful impact. In our view, goal setting does at least four things that contribute to high levels of productivity.

Goals Foster a Sense of Individual Responsibility

The sense of individual responsibility is probably the single most important thing that goal setting accomplishes.

Take some time to talk to people who have been remarkably successful and you will notice that the overwhelming majority of them accept personal responsibility for what they have accomplished. You might think that their willingness to accept responsibility is just a way of bragging. But if you talk to them long enough you will notice that they accept responsibility for both their successes and their "failures." We put the word failures in quotation marks because many successful people don't think about failures. Instead, they talk about "learning experiences." There is a world of difference between the two phrases; you may want to take a minute or two to reflect on it.

Similarly, you might want to talk to some people who are dissatisfied with their lives. If you talk long enough you will discover that they seldom accept responsibility for the things that have happened to them. Listen to some examples.

I wanted to go to college but my parents couldn't afford it.

I wanted to open my own business but the bank wouldn't loan me the money.

I almost won but the other guy cheated.

I could have been a great athlete, but my parents wouldn't let me play sports.

Each of these stories could be true: many parents can't afford to send their children to college, banks regularly refuse to make loans, some people break the rules, and many parents won't allow their children to participate in sports. The important thing is that these people have let problems become obstacles; they let the problems prevent them from accomplishing what they set out to do. They also focus too much on the barriers from the past and assume that they are permanent. In contrast, really successful people find ways to solve their problems. They focus on the future. Rather than figuring out what was to blame, they focus on how to solve the problem. They get things done in spite of obstacles. Goals encourage high levels of performance by helping people accept responsibility for their own achievements, instead of shifting that responsibility onto the problems they encounter along the way.

Goals Focus Attention and Effort

The second thing that goals do for us is probably almost as important as the first.

We live in a complex and exciting world. Countless people and activities compete for our time. Think of the number of things you could do on a casual Saturday away from work. If your list is anything like ours it probably includes some of the following activities: swimming, bicycling, shopping, walking along the beach, visiting friends, going to a movie, washing the car, doing some work around the house, preparing for class, grading student papers, reading a book, watching TV, attending a sporting event, stopping by a gym to work out, going on a picnic, or just sitting around recovering from a busy week. And, as if we didn't already have enough to think about, skilled advertisers constantly introduce new ways to spend our time and money.

Where we live we may have more choices than people in other parts of the country, but the object lesson is the same: *if you don't take charge of your own time, someone else will.* Goals are the single best means we know of for ordering your time because they help you focus on the things that are really important to you.

THERE IS ALWAYS TIME FOR WHAT'S IMPORTANT!

Goals Improve Decision Making

This point is closely related to the last one. Just as you make choices about your time and effort, you also make choices about countless other elements in your life: which car to buy, how much to spend on groceries, which college to attend, where to go on vacation, who to go out with, whether or not to buy a magazine subscription, which job offer to accept, which project to work on.

We could add to our list of decisions just by keeping track of the things we do in a single day. In fact, you might want to try keeping such a list if you have never done it before. Most people are surprised by the number of choices they make every day. And because they aren't conscious of the decisions they make, many people squander their resources by making decisions that are inconsistent with their objectives.

Here is the really important point: *every decision you make in a typical day is an opportunity to move you closer to success.* But this is a double-edged sword. Every decision you make also has the risk of moving you further away from your objectives. How do you make sure that you are making the right decisions? Simple, by checking each decision against your goals. Of course you will still make some mistakes—everyone does. But if you take the time to consider every major decision in terms of its impact on your goals, you have a much better chance of making decisions that consistently bring you closer to success.

Goals Provide a Record of Achievement on Which to Build New Expectations

The final value of goal setting is one that emerges over time. As you work with goals, you begin to see your life transformed. Little by little, day by day you create a record of success that builds on itself. You feel better about yourself when you see what you've accomplished. Friends and family members value you more because of your achievements. And employers and potential employers are more likely to recognize your merit because you can point to a constantly growing string of accomplishments.

Financial goals are important to many people. Just "getting by" tops the list for some of us. Others have more expansive goals. Buying a new house, sending a child to college, saving for a special vacation, and preparing for retirement are also financial goals.

Accomplishing these goals requires careful attention to personal and professional budgeting. You can use pencil and paper to prepare a budget and monitor your income and expenses. There is nothing wrong with that approach and people have used it for hundreds of years.

However, paper and pencil systems are often so time consuming that many people give up or rely on best guesses. Fortunately, a new generation of computer programs takes much of the drudgery out of budgeting. These programs make life easier and make it possible for you to be much more precise than with other methods.

Quicken, a leading personal financial management program, is like an electronic checkbook, but it does much more than you would expect any checkbook to do.

Release 3.0 is the newest and most powerful version and it includes a number of features that even make it possible to manage a small business. In addition to organizing your financial records and helping you track your expenses, *Quicken* can write checks, record credit card charges, prepare cash flow and balance statements, and provide detailed reports of taxable income and deductible expenses.

Quicken runs on IBM PCs and fully compatible computers with 320 K RAM, DOS 2.0 or higher, and one or more floppy disk drives or a hard disk. *Quicken* is currently available from Intuit; 66 Willow Place; Menlo Park, CA 94025-3687; (415) 322-2800; for $60.

SETTING B.E.S.T. GOALS

Goal setting is an extremely powerful technique. You probably know of several books about goal setting, and you may have even read one or two. Recently several companies have produced audio and video taped instructional packages on goal setting. So you may wonder why some people fail in spite of having set goals. There can be a number of causes. We have met people who spend more time talking about their goals than working on them. And I think everyone has had the experience of setting New Year's resolutions that are forgotten the next day.

Although it is never fun to look at someone else's shortcomings, it is instructive to consider why so many well-meaning people have failed in spite of their goals. More often than not, the things they called goals were incomplete or poorly formed—call them "pseudo goals" if you like. The important point is that although the person called them goals, they had little impact on the person's day to day activities. To be effective, goals must be formed so that they provide guidance, day in and day out. Goals are not something to be written and put away; they have to be living, breathing guidelines that shape our lives as we work to accomplish them.

Let's take a brief look at someone who is doomed to fail. It's not a pretty picture but it helps to show what we mean. John Marshall—not his real name—is a high school teacher in an Eastern city. John enjoys teaching and works hard at his job. Although he looks successful to most people, those who know him well know he is deeply dissatisfied. All of John's close friends have heard him talk about the things he would like to accomplish. He would like to build a new home for his family, and his dreams include a summer home and sailboat on a mountain lake a few hundred miles away. He regularly talks about how much he would like to travel and he is often near the front of the line when new exotic sports cars are unveiled. Yes, there is a lot John would like to do and have, but teachers barely earn a fraction of what his dreams would cost. When asked where he is going to get the money, John's answers have a familiar ring. "Oh, I don't know," he says, "I guess I'll have to get out of teaching and go to work in business someday." And that's about as far as anyone ever goes with John because he becomes decidedly unpleasant if someone asks him *when* all this is going to happen.

Why is John doomed to failure? Because he has never taken the time to turn his daydreams into concrete goals. Goals are more than daydreams. They are linked to concrete action steps that build logically to the outcome a person would like. Goals help you to do your best. In fact, the word "best" is a convenient way to remember the things about goals that can help you change old habits and start turning your dreams into reality. To be effective, your goals must be Believable, Energizing, Specific, and Timed.

B.E.S.T. Goals Are Believable

Believability is the most important feature of goals. Unless you believe, really believe, that you can accomplish what you set out to do, goal setting is wasted. It doesn't matter what anyone else thinks, but you must believe that you can do it. In fact, many of humanity's most stunning feats have been accomplished by people everyone else thought were nuts. Examples come to mind readily: the Golden Gate Bridge, the Wright brothers' airplane, the Apple computer. The important point about these examples is that the people working on them believed in themselves—in spite of what everyone else said.

If you are new to goal setting, you may not have much confidence in yourself. Quitting smoking, losing a few pounds, or buying a new home may seem as far away as walking on the moon. The easiest way to get over this hurdle is to start small. Pick a few small tasks that will help you build toward your ultimate goal. For example, you may not believe you can quit smoking or lose a few pounds, but you can get started by reading the most recent literature from the American Heart Society. Similarly, you may not believe you can save enough money for a down payment on a new home, but you can get in the habit of saving by putting aside a few dollars a week.

Once you begin setting and achieving goals, no matter how small, you will begin to get a sense of your own power. Get in the habit of setting goals and you can begin setting ever larger, more challenging goals for yourself. In fact, goal setting is a process that builds upon itself. Like a weight lifter who begins with a goal of lifting 100 pounds and gradually increases his goals to 110, 120, 130, 140 pounds, your belief in yourself will grow as you build on a record of accomplishment.

Remember to set realistic goals, but don't sell yourself short. There's nothing wrong with difficult goals. Just make sure to build in smaller goals, or milestones that you can meet along the way. These help you know if you're getting there. Build in rewards along the way, too. Remember, life is a process, not an end result.

B.E.S.T. Goals Are Energizing

The energy they can provide is the second important feature of goals. Properly developed goals are the "spark" that gets you started in the morning. There may always be days when you just don't feel like getting out of bed. And we all find ourselves in situations where nothing seems to go right. Goals really matter at such times. Goals can be the "jump start" that gets you out of the jam and moving again.

Goals can provide this kind of energy when they are tied to things that matter to you. The most important thing is that they do matter to you. Things that matter to other people—family, friends, coworkers, etc.—may motivate them, but only things that matter to you can energize you. You can expect goals to be a source of energy as long as they are linked to things that you value. Whatever is important to you—home, family, car, job, free time—your goals should be directly related to things you value.

People occasionally have difficulty identifying what matters most to them. If you are in that spot, or if you simply want to double check your gut feelings, take a moment to complete the following exercise.

The following list describes things that many people value. Read the list once to make sure you understand each term.

_____   a comfortable home

_____   a life of adventure and excitement

_____   a stable, orderly life

_____   security; being sure that nothing will happen to upset your life

_____   freedom and independence

_____   respect, knowing that people look up to you

_____   companionship, close friends with whom you can discuss your experiences

_____   intellectual growth; mastering new fields

_____   feelings of accomplishment; knowing that you have done important things

_____   a world of beauty; being surrounded by works of art

_____   personal expression; being able to do and say things that come from "deep inside" you

Use the extra spaces to add any terms or phrases that come to mind as you read the list.

_____

_____

_____

_____

Now, read the list a second time and mark each item with the following code:

A = something deeply important to me
B = something I respect in others but don't need to do myself
C = something of no interest

Set your list aside for a day or two before undertaking the final step.

When you come back to this project, reread your list and ask yourself What kind of person is this? What is it like to be him/her? What does he/she like to do? How does he/she spend time? What should I do to become this person?

You may even write a brief description of this person. Or, if you want to carry things a step further, write a brief letter introducing yourself to this person. Describe who you are, what you like about yourself, and what you are doing to become more like this person.

B.E.S.T. Goals Are Specific

Goals are specific when they are defined so precisely that you can see what it will be like to achieve them. In fact, the more specific you can be, the more likely you are to achieve the goal. Although many people say they would like to be successful, few people can say exactly what that means. For some people, titles are the mark of success. For other people, success is measured by their income. Still other people think in terms of professional recognition, personal accomplishments, social stature, or education. Whatever success means to you, your goals should be defined in terms of specific accomplishments that constitute success.

What does it mean to be "successful?" The way you define success is entirely personal. The thing to remember is that you have to define it in terms of specific accomplishments to make your goal meaningful.

Goals that are specific help you focus your attention on the things you need to do to accomplish them. They also help you see when you are "on track" and when you need to devote additional effort. For example, suppose you set a goal to save $1200 over the next year. That is an ideal goal because you will know when you have achieved it and you will also know whether or not you are making needed progress. You could plan to save approximately $100 every month, and you could keep track of your progress by looking at the balance in your savings account at the month's end. After the first month, you have saved $95. Not bad, but a little short of where you need to be. The balance at the end of the second month is $199. Again, not bad but still a little short. At the end of the third month, a balance of $325 says that you are ahead of schedule. A graph, like the one in Figure 1.1, can help you track your progress.

Saving $1200 in a year is an easy goal to make specific because dollars and time are conventional sources of measurement. Fortunately, there are ways to measure almost everything else we do. Whether you want to lose weight, read books, increase the number of clients that use your services, or just spend more time having fun, there are ways to measure and record your progress. Even complex projects can be broken down into several steps, and the techniques introduced in the next chapter make it easy to keep track of milestones in any project.

B.E.S.T. Goals Are Timed

Finally, time limits make the difference between goals and daydreams. We have even heard people describe goals as "daydreams with deadlines." Deadlines help keep you on track and they may provide the extra push you need. Learning to set time limits may be one of the hardest things about goal setting.

Figure 1.1 Tracking Critical Success Factors

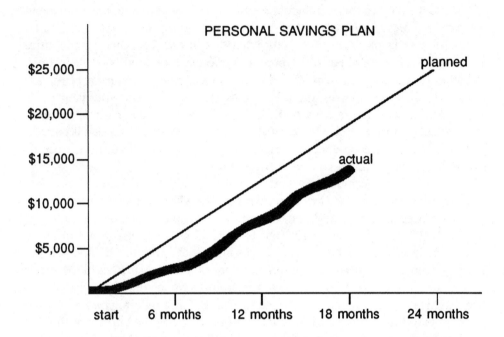

Time limits that are reasonable for one goal may be ridiculously easy for another and impossibly demanding for others. Sometimes you can accomplish a great deal very quickly when everything falls into place. At other times, you may see very little progress over long periods of time because there are so many obstacles.

Time limits also help you discover your dependencies. These are the elements or people you need to achieve your goals. Goals cannot be achieved in a vacuum. For us to do things, we often need other people to do things, so that still other people can do things, and so on, and so on, and so on. . . . You'll find that many of your time frames depend on other people's time frames. So you need to build them into your plan.

Ultimately, you will learn by trial and error. The best advice we can give you is to keep track of your goals and the progress you are making. Write your goals in a workbook or diary and take time every week to see how close you've come. As you learn more about yourself and your goals, you will get better and better at planning.

We have described B.E.S.T. goals as they apply to your personal life. In a minute you will see that they can also be used in business. But we need to introduce one more concept first: critical success factors.

SETTING GOALS AT WORK: CRITICAL SUCCESS FACTORS

So far we have talked about goals in personal contexts. We've done that deliberately because the concepts come alive when we think of them in personal terms. However, this doesn't mean that their importance is limited to personal contexts. In fact, goals are particularly powerful in professional settings.

Think of some of the successful professionals you know. If they have shared with you much about their lives, most of them probably talked about their goals. Examples that come to my mind include the president of a six billion dollar corporation talking about financial goals for the next year, and the president of a small consulting firm who responds to problems by saying "It looks like we have some goals to set."

Goal setting is almost second nature for many successful professionals. This is hardly surprising because goal setting is such a powerful way of focusing attention on things that matter. However, a factor that complicates goal setting at work is inability to identify the goals. Most of us know what really matters in our personal lives. With a little help—like the dream vacation exercise—most of us can outline the things of greatest importance to us. Unfortunately, it's not quite so easy to set goals in professional settings. There may be so many people involved and so much may be happening that it is often difficult to identify the things that make a difference between success and failure. Worse yet, every business may be different and each company may have its own objectives.

Standard financial reports provide a wealth of information about any company and its operations. Unfortunately, these reports are designed for regulators and sophisticated investors. Balance sheets and income statements document a company's performance, but they seldom present information in a manner that answers the needs of operations managers. Accounting conventions, generally accepted principles, and reporting standards require specialized vocabularies that often mean little to nonfinancial executives.

We have frequently heard managers make disparaging statements about "financial mumbo jumbo," often accompanied by dramatic gestures, as current financial statements are filed—one way or the other. Managers often do the best they can and hope that the "numbers will be OK," while making decisions on other grounds.

During the 1950s, Louis R. Mobley, Director of the IBM Executive School, recognized the need to translate information from standard financial reports into forms that would be meaningful to operating executives. His goal was to create a system that any nonfinancial executive, CEO, or entrepreneur could use to understand the complete financial picture of the company.

Drawing concepts from the world-class faculty at the IBM Executive School, Mobley developed a unique approach to financial education. Mobley's system combines information from standard financial reports with interpretive formulas to guide managers making business decisions.

Following his retirement, Mobley continued to refine his system and worked with associates to develop commercial applications. While consulting with profit and not-for-profit organizations, Mobley and associates developed a powerful system that explains financial performance in terms nonfinancial managers can understand.

The system Mobley and his associates developed is now available commercially in Version 2.0 of *The Mobley Matrix*. In its current form, *Matrix* does far more than help managers interpret financial data. *Matrix* helps managers focus on critical success factors by linking business decisions and actions to financial results. With *Matrix*, executives can manage the future by doing "what-if" tests of alternate strategies to improve the quality of their business decisions.

Information may be entered directly into *Matrix* or imported from accounting packages or spread sheets. Information for any period is displayed in a "Results Matrix" combining the beginning balance sheet, balance sheet adjustments, income statement, cash statement, and ending balance sheet.

Strategies are developed and tested in the "Strategies Screen." This view analyzes and forecasts information in twelve categories including sales, cash flows, credit ratios, and return on investment. The *Matrix* "Map" lets you move forward and backward in time, with a few simple key strokes. This makes it easy to predict results of various strategies over, time while graphs generated by the *Matrix* display numerous performance measures.

The Mobley Matrix runs on IBM PC and fully compatible computers with at least 640K RAM, DOS 2.0 or higher, and a hard disk. *Matrix* is currently available from Mobley Matrix International, Inc.; 12555 W. Jefferson Boulevard, Suite 204; Los Angeles, CA 90066; (213) 207-5310 or (800) 777-8181, for $895.

Researchers from several fields have studied problems caused by the complexity of business settings. An especially useful approach has been developed by scholars working on information systems who simplify professional situations by focusing on critical success factors.

Briefly, a critical success factor is anything that an organization or person must do well in order to be successful. The advantage in focusing on critical success factors is that usually there are relatively few of them. Of all the things that a manager might worry about, the critical success factors are the few things that really make a difference.

Things that are critical success factors in one organization may not matter in other organizations. Even within one organization the critical success factors at one level may be unimportant to people at another level. Let's look at a couple of examples.

Karen owns a small shoe store in a large shopping center. She used to spend a lot of money on advertising, but she stopped when she realized that the money was probably wasted. Lots of people come to the mall every day, and all Karen needs to do is make sure they stop at her store. Now she concentrates on three things that seem to make a difference: (1) eye-catching displays, (2) a clean, inviting entrance, and (3) courteous employees.

Carol supervises several secretaries in the word processing pool of a large company. At first she spent lots of time worrying about the things each person did. For example, she tried to keep careful records showing when each person arrived in the morning, how long they took for lunch, how many breaks they took, when they went home in the evening, and how much time they spent on the phone. This is only a partial list, but you get the idea. It didn't take her long to realize that she was spending so much time keeping track of what everyone did that she didn't have time to worry about the results. Now she keeps track of two things: amount of work produced, and number of complaints from the people they work for. She knows that everything is OK as long as they are getting the work out and their customers are satisfied.

John coaches a Little League baseball team. He used to worry a lot about his win-loss record, and he was constantly frustrated because so many things were out of his control. Now he concentrates on getting his players to practice and making sure they work hard. He knows that he will win his share of games as long as his players practice hard.

Setting and managing goals is as important in business as in personal affairs. The hard part has always been figuring out what a manager should concentrate on.

Most managers have learned through trial and error—through "hard experience," many say. Learning through trial and error is effective, but it can be expensive. Errors can be costly enough to put a small business out of business, and successes may be hard to duplicate.

Now computer simulations provide a convenient way to learn without the costs of trial and error. Computer simulations have been around for many years, but most required such large computers that it was impractical to use them on anything less than a mainframe. Fortunately, the increasing power of personal computers—and the growing skill of programmers—has made it possible for many individual users to work with powerful simulations.

Venture magazine's *Business Simulator* is one of our favorites. With *Business Simulator*, you direct a simulated company through five phases: start-up, growth, independence, new product development, and new market development. Competing with industry giants, you review economic conditions, industry statistics, stock and bond reports, corporate earnings, and sales and inventory figures as you make decisions about marketing, finance, and operations. The quality of your decisions determines the fate of your company.

Years of trial and error are compressed to a few hours. Learning is facilitated by a pop-up tutorial that explains business terms and concepts. A built-in consultant provides advice and a helpful analysis feature makes it easy to compare your performance with your competitors.

Advanced users will enjoy the built-in case studies that represent different corporate scenarios. For example, "Innovate" places users at the helm of a company which has been a market leader but has begun losing sales.

Business Simulator runs on IBM PC and fully compatible computers with 256K RAM and two disk drives or a hard disk. The Macintosh version requires 512K RAM and two 800K disk drives or a hard disk. *Business Simulator* is currently available from Strategic Management Group, Inc.; 3624 Market Street; University City Science Center; Philadelphia, PA 19104; (800) 445-7089; for $69.95.

Most of us can relate to these examples easily. You should know that even senior managers find it useful to concentrate on critical success factors. Moreover, all members of an organization should be able to identify critical success factors for their particular positions. Let's look at one more example to make this point.

Mark is the general manager of a large hotel. With over 1700 rooms, nearly 2000 employees, 3 restaurants, and 2 bars, there are lots of things he could worry about. Fortunately, Mark's objective is clearly defined (to earn a profit), and he knows what makes a difference in his operations. He watches the occupancy statistics, average room rate, number of meals served, and quantity of alcohol poured. If these measures are on target, Mark knows he will make a profit. When any of these numbers fall off, Mark knows whom to see.

In addition, each of the people who work for Mark know what things they have to watch. For example, Carol supervises the front desk where people check in. There are a handful of things she watches: number of people waiting in line, average length of time it takes each person to check in, and how often a desk clerk needs to call a supervisor for help.

Finally, Carla is a new desk clerk working for Carol. Carla knows that she needs to check in each guest and answer any questions in 4.5 minutes, on the average, making errors on fewer than 5 percent of transactions.

We could extend this example by looking at the critical success factors for everyone who works in the hotel. But this should be enough to show you how critical success factors work in a complex organization. Each person from the bottom to the top knows what their responsibilities are, and each knows what factors tell them whether or not they are successful.

Now here is the point: when you set goals in a professional environment, focus on the critical success factors for your job and responsibilities. You will need to rely on your knowledge of your job and your company's objectives, but you can follow a relatively simple procedure. The first question to ask yourself is "What are we doing this for?" In the case of the coach, it was the process that mattered. In the case of the others, it was the outcome. As obvious as this seems, we often get caught up in a tangent of measuring the wrong thing. Some people measure the process when they really need to know the outcome, and others do just the reverse. It reminds us of the story of the tourist in Ireland who asked a local fellow how to get to another town. The local resident, upon hearing the query said, "Laddie, if I was agoin' there, I wouldn't be startin' from here." Think about it.

CONCLUSION: USING CRITICAL SUCCESS FACTORS TO SET GOALS

We have introduced two important concepts in this chapter: B.E.S.T. goals, and critical success factors. We want you to realize that these two concepts can be made to work together in both business and personal contexts.

Critical success factors represent the areas in which you ought to set goals. Here is a simple, four-step procedure that you can use to set goals for any activity.

Step 1: Identify the Critical Success Factors

You can always ask others for help with this, but there is really no substitute for your own knowledge and experience. Just ask yourself which differences make a difference. You may want to review our discussion of critical success factors. Focus on three or four key issues.

Step 2: Determine Current Levels of Performance

This step establishes the base line or foundation for goal setting. For each of the critical success factors you have identified, pick an appropriate measurement and record your current level of performance. Don't make judgments. These measurements are neither good nor bad; they just form your starting point.

Step 3: Set B.E.S.T. Goals

Many people prefer to shoot from the hip here but we think you need to set reasonable expectations. As you gain experience, it will be easier to set reasonable goals for yourself. However, its probably wise to aim for small improvements at first, and grow into bigger things later. Matching competitors' standards may be your first step. After you have gotten on track you can work on becoming the best.

Step 4: Keep Track of Your Performance

Finally, monitor your performance. Once you know where you began and where you are going, its easy to graph your progress. This way you know when you are on schedule and can coast a bit, and you know when you are behind schedule and need to work a bit harder. Figure 1.1 shows a friend's savings plan. Graphs like this are a handy way to keep track of progress.

SUGGESTED READINGS

Bower, Joseph L. and Thomas M. Hout. "Fast-Cycle Capability for Competitive Power." *Harvard Business Review* (November-December 1988): 110–18.

Byrne, John A. "Don't Let Time Management Be A Waste of Time." *Business Week*, 4 May 1987, 144.

Dorney, Robert C. "Making Time to Manage." *Harvard Business Review* (January-February 1988): 38–40.

Mackenzie, Alec. *Time For Success*. New York: McGraw-Hill Publishing Company, 1989.

Stalk, George, Jr. "Time—The Next Source of Competitive Advantage." *Harvard Business Review* (July-August 1988): 41–51.

Thomas, Philip R. "Executive Weaponry: Short Cycle Times Slay Competitors." *Electronic Business*, 6 March 1989, 116–19.

Worthy, Ford S. "How CEOs Manage Their Time." *Fortune*, 18 January 1988, 88–92.

Chapter 2

ORGANIZING YOUR LIFE

PROJECT MANAGEMENT
AT HOME AND AT WORK

John is like many of the professionals we meet in our seminars. He is bright, and his superiors consider him "very promising." Just three years out of school, John has moved through the ranks at his company much faster than usual.

Things have gone well for John, but he now finds himself with a problem—a serious problem that he doesn't know quite how to handle. You might call his situation a "crisis," but John doesn't like the way that sounds. Instead, he says that he is experiencing some "career difficulty," and is looking for ways to deal with it.

When John first came to us, we began by offering him some reassurance. His problem is like that of many other professionals. You may be able to identify with some elements.

A COMMON PROBLEM

John's problem began when he was promoted to a managerial position. In a nutshell, John is having difficulty taking responsibility for scheduling his own work and setting deadlines for himself. Although it may sound strange, this is the first time in his life that John has had to take responsibility for himself.

John's parents had set some big goals for him, and they had always been there to make sure he was on track. When he moved on to school, John got used to other people scheduling his work. Teachers set deadlines for his school work, while his friends and parents planned many of the events in his personal life.

Even after John graduated, other people scheduled things for him. That was especially important at work. His bosses told him what had to be done and when it needed to be finished. If he had difficulty meeting a deadline, there was always someone there to help him sort out his priorities.

John thrived in the controlled atmosphere. In fact, much of his success resulted from his ability to meet deadlines set by others. Now John is in trouble because he has never learned to plan his own work. And he has virtually no experience doing the kinds of things that every manager needs to do: setting deadlines, establishing priorities, and scheduling activities.

John is in over his head, and it is beginning to show in his work. His life seems to be one problem after another. He is so busy trying to get out of trouble—"fighting one fire after another"—that he never has time to get ahead of the game. John's supervisor has had a number of "heart-to-heart" talks with him, but the problems keep recurring.

Knowing that he is in trouble, John has worked hard to get a handle on his job. He has read a couple of books on time management, attended a few seminars, and even bought one of the popular notebook schedulers advertised as the solution to everyone's time management problems. These things have helped a bit, but in John's own words "they seem like a bunch of gimmicks. They help for a while but then I get right back into the rut. Work piles up and I go on crisis footing for a while. As soon as I'm over the peak, I'm so tired that I simply collapse until the next crisis hits."

TAKING CHARGE: GETTING OFF THE ROLLER COASTER

John has a lot in common with many other professionals we have met. They are making a major transition by accepting responsibility for scheduling their lives. Setting goals and keeping track of progress is the first step, but many remain overwhelmed. Their lives seem to be on a roller coaster: peak demands alternating with periods of exhaustion. They are so tired from the peaks that they can't use the valleys to get ahead of the game. Above all else, they need a way to get off the roller coaster. The ideal solution would be a way to balance their work loads, a way to even out the peaks and valleys.

This chapter introduces a way to get off the roller coaster. We call it project management, but don't let the name get in your way.

In our seminars, we tell people that project management is the single most important thing they can do to organize their personal and professional lives. Goal setting helps people decide what they would like to accomplish, but project management helps them figure out how to get it done. Of course, both are important and you don't need to choose between the two approaches. In fact, a rigorous program of goal setting makes it easier to use project management, because you always know where you are going. And project management makes it easier to pursue your goals, because you always know where you stand in the process.

The first half of this chapter will introduce a project management approach to organizing personal and professional tasks. The second half of the chapter will help you create a personal scheduler that is more powerful than many of the commercial systems that sell for hundreds of dollars. Together, the project management approach and personal scheduler will help you get organized so that you can focus your time and attention on the things that really matter in your life.

PROJECT MANAGEMENT

Everybody manages projects. According to researchers, there are five things that distinguish projects from other activities. Looking at the list you will probably find that much of what you do involves managing projects.

1. Projects are unique, one-time activities. Things that we do again and again, day in and day out are ongoing activities. Projects are things we start and finish. Then we move on to new projects.

2. Projects use limited resources. The resources may be time, money, manpower, or anything else that is in short supply. Projects aim to make the best use of the resources we are given.

3. Projects have a specific goal or purpose. This goal is important because it tells us why we are doing something and tells us when we are finished.

4. Projects involve a sequence of activities. There are always several different steps and some of them must be done before others can be started.

5. Projects take place in a defined period of time. There is always a start date and a deadline, a point in time by which the project needs to be finished.

Because much of what we do is really project management, it makes sense to use some of the approaches that have been developed over the last few years. Unfortunately, many people are confused by the term "project management."

Some people think project management is as simple as keeping a to-do list. To them, project management is so simple that there is nothing to learn. They may even have elaborate lists headed CURRENT PROJECTS and they frequently complain that things don't get done in spite of their efforts.

Other people think of project management as hopelessly complicated—so complicated that they could never learn to use the systems. These people may have seen some of the elaborate tools used to manage complex projects. They have heard about Gantt charts, pert diagrams, and critical path method (CPM) schedules. And they may even be familiar with massive computer programs capable of handling exhaustive lists of resources, thousands of tasks, millions of dollars, and hundreds of people.

The unfortunate thing is that both groups of people—those who think of project management as keeping a list and those who think of project management as terribly complicated—are prevented from taking advantage of some fairly simple approaches that would make their lives much easier. We believe that project management doesn't have to be complicated. We have seen some fairly simple approaches make an enormous difference in people's lives. And we believe project management is an essential skill.

AN OVERVIEW OF PROJECT MANAGEMENT

Let's start by looking at an example. Almost everyone we know has had to write a report at some time in their lives. Students write reports as class assignments, managers write reports for higher management, and most professionals write reports—and proposals—for clients.

Report writing is such a commonplace activity that few people think of it as a project. However, writing a report has all the earmarks of a project. First, each report is a unique, one-time activity. A person may have to write several reports, but each is a distinct task. And when each report is finished, its author moves on to other projects.

Second, writing a report uses limited resources. For most people, the limited resources are the writer's time and knowledge. Other limitations may include dollars allocated for research, the capacity of word processing systems, and regulations limiting the disclosure of information.

Third, there is a distinct purpose or goal for writing the report. Passing a course, summarizing some research, getting approval for another project, and satisfying a client are all worthwhile purposes. Notice the goal or purpose is the reason for writing the report. If it weren't for the specific goal or purpose, the report would never be written.

Fourth, writing a report involves a sequence of activities. Most people go through the critical steps of analyzing their assignment, summarizing what they already know, doing additional research, composing a draft, editing the draft, preparing final copy, and submitting the report. Some of these steps—editing, for example—may be repeated several times. But each is a distinct step and it makes sense to do them in an orderly fashion.

Finally, reports are written during a defined period of time. The process begins when the report is assigned and ends when the report is submitted, hopefully before the deadline. Even when working on their own, professionals need to set deadlines so they can get on with other projects.

Escaping Activity Traps

Writing a report is usually a pretty simple project. Most people have done it many times. That makes it a good example for our purposes. While writing reports, most people have encountered activity traps. For example, some students get so involved in conducting research that they leave too little time for writing and editing. Frequently the result is a hastily composed report in which no one takes pride, submitted after the deadline.

We believe activity traps are enormous obstacles to higher levels of productivity. They are everywhere, so you need to be sensitive to them. Let's look at a few examples.

Steve is a clerk in a popular sporting goods store. The store is frequently crowded, so management has instituted a take-a-number system. People waiting for help take a number and clerks call numbers in order to make sure that customers are waited on in turn. The problem is that Steve requires everyone to take a number, even when no one else is waiting.

Mary is a program manager for a civil engineering firm. She has had the job for two years and has developed a sophisticated job-costing and proposal-writing system. Even on multi-million dollar jobs, her estimates are accurate to within a few dollars. Unfortunately, the job-costing system takes so long that her bids are seldom submitted on time. As a result, her company has begun to lose many of the projects on which she works.

Karl supervises the maintenance crew in a small commercial printing plant. His job includes assigning the mechanics who help machine operators set up each new press run. Karl learned early that some mechanics and press operators work well together and some do not. He is very careful to think through each assignment, taking into account the strengths and weaknesses of each person. Lately his boss has noticed that the mechanics spend a lot of time standing around while Karl decides who is best for each job.

Carla is one of the most conscientious Composition teachers in her district. She has a reputation for doing everything right, and she believes grading is one of her most important tasks. Students can't grow, she says, unless they know exactly what they are doing right and what they need to do to improve. Working from this philosophy, Carla has devised an elaborate grading system. Each paper is graded on a seven point scale in twelve distinct areas. Carla's master record lists each student's grade in each category on each assignment. Unfortunately, her students make below average progress because she is seldom able to return graded essays before the next round is due.

As a result, her students often end up guessing what they should do while waiting for her feedback.

These examples may sound extreme, but all of them are taken from real life. And all point to the same problem: activity traps. Each of the participants is so busy doing a task that they have lost sight of the reason for it. If nothing else, a project management system should help you avoid this problem.

An Ideal System

If you were to design your own project management system, you would probably want one that helps you plan your work, avoid activity traps, make sure you don't leave out important steps, and never miss a deadline. Those were the objectives we set for ourselves, and we think we have come close.

Our system uses a planning sheet for each project and a summary sheet for keeping track of several projects at once. The following pages include several examples and samples of each that you may want to copy for your own use.

The Project Planning Sheet

Project planning sheets are the core of our system. You should develop one for each project you manage. The following example shows a project planning sheet developed by a product champion in a fast cycle manufacturing company. Beginning with her own observations and a few casual conversations with friends, she developed the concept for a new product. She hopes to have the product on the shelves of retail stores in time for the next Christmas rush.

GOAL: the personal valet is to be on the market in time for sale next Christmas.

FINISHED PRODUCT: the personal valet will be a portable office including a calendar, calculator, and desk tools in a standard-sized leather notebook selling for no more than $25 retail.

PROJECT SUMMARY/TARGET DATES:
26 November	product shelved for sale in 2500 retail outlets
15 November	formal product release
15 October	prelaunch advertising
15 July	prototype product available for review
15 April	final design review
1 March	formal assembly of product team
15 February	presentation to senior management

If you can't identify with introduction of a new product, take a look at the planning sheet for a typical student report. Take time to examine it before reading the discussion of each part.

GOAL: to get an A in History.

FINISHED PRODUCT/DEADLINE: a 5 to 7 page report on the 1929 stock market crash turned in by March 17; the finished report must use at least five reference works including one general economics textbook.

PROJECT SUMMARY/TARGET DATES:

~~10 February~~   ~~reread chapter in Economics 101 text~~
~~12 February~~   ~~get four reference books from the library~~
~~20 February~~   ~~read and take notes on the four additional reference~~
                  ~~works~~
~~24 February~~   ~~compile notes and prepare outline~~
~~1 March~~   ~~compose rough draft~~
5 March   revise rough draft
7 March   type revised draft
12 March   edit revised draft
15 March   type final draft

This is a pretty typical project planning. There are several important features to consider.

The first thing you should notice is that the entire project is outlined on a single sheet. You can see the entire project outline in a single glance, and you never lose sight of your objectives.

Of course, some projects are far more complex than these. You may be tempted to create far more elaborate multi-page project management sheets so you can detail every step of the project. We agree that detailed outlines are valuable, but we still think it's important to be able to see the whole at a glance.

If you really feel the need to create more detailed outlines, you might try dividing the overall project into several smaller or partial projects. For example, you might break "read and take notes on the four additional reference works" into several smaller pieces: read and take notes on reference work one, read and take notes on reference work two, and so forth. As long as the detailed breakdown will fit on one page, everything is OK. If the detailed breakdown won't fit on a single page, try setting up a separate project sheet for each reference work.

The personal or professional goal is the next thing you ought to notice. Strictly speaking, the goal is not part of the project, but listing it with the project has a very important psychological function. Major projects take lots of time and effort. Even minor setbacks can be frustrating, and everyone has days when nothing seems to go right. If you keep your eyes fixed on the goal, you will have the drive you need to get through periods of frustration.

It is also important to look at the way the finished product is described. Notice that it is depicted as a tangible thing, a physical object, completed by a deadline. That is important because it helps you avoid activity traps.

Time and again, we have seen people get in trouble by describing projects in terms of activities. Writing a report can be an endless activity. So can designing a building, hiring a secretary, and developing a client. These may be worthwhile projects, but you stand a much better chance of completing them if you concentrate on the finished product, the thing you are creating.

Finally, look at the project summary. Notice that each of the major steps is listed in a logical order with a target date. Those that have been completed are crossed out, so it is easy to see where you are in the project. And it is easy to see whether or not you are on schedule. If you are right on time, you can keep working at your regular pace. If you are ahead of schedule, you can relax a bit and devote more attention to other projects. But if you are behind, you know you need to put more time and effort into this project. This can also alert you to situations in which you need more help or need to revise your plan.

Project management is a powerful tool for organizing time. Small projects can be managed with nothing more than the paper and pencil techniques described in the text. However, larger more complex projects frequently require more sophisticated approaches.

Project management software for personal computers has been available for several years. All good project management programs will:

- help you break complex projects into smaller tasks or jobs,
- organize tasks into the order they must be executed,
- identify critical paths—the most time sensitive jobs that can delay the entire project if they are not completed on schedule,
- prepare graphs and diagrams showing relationships between individual tasks, and
- update plans to compare work completed with that planned.

More sophisticated programs let you manage more tasks, generate improved graphs and diagrams, coordinate more resources, identify potential trouble spots, and analyze budgets. Of course, additional features are not free—these programs cost more and require more sophisticated computers.

Our favorite project management programs represent two clearly defined price-performance categories.

PS5 is among the more sophisticated project management programs for personal computers. *PS5* can handle up to 2000 jobs per project and 500 resource classifications. There are no limits to the number of projects in memory, resources per job, or predecessors per job. The built-in calendar tracks dates from 1980 through 2019.

Carefully designed menus and commands guide you through the process of creating and updating project plans. When you create a project plan, you begin by assigning a name and start date. You can use a built-in calendar to define work and nonwork days, and a separate screen invites you to identify the resources you will commit to the project.

Listing specific jobs or tasks is the next step. A simple template is used to enter each task, and you can indicate how long each one will take and when it can begin. If you make a mistake it's easy to go back to edit tasks you have already entered, and you can always add more tasks.

Once you have entered all of the tasks, it's time to show how they fit together. *PS5* really shines here. Using a mouse, you can physically move boxes representing each task and draw connecting lines to show which jobs must be finished before others can be started. When you have finished moving and connecting jobs, a click of the mouse or touch of function keys lets you toggle back and forth between network diagrams and Gantt charts.

You can update your project plans whenever you like, and print a variety of reports showing overall progress and resource allocations. You can take a break whenever you like because *PS5* saves all of the files associated with a project and reloads them when you call up the project again.

PS5 runs on an IBM PC and fully compatible computers with DOS 3.0 or higher, 512K RAM, a hard disk, and graphics adapter. A mouse and printer or plotter are highly recommended options. *PS5* is currently available from Scitor Corporation; 393 Vintage Park Drive; Suite 140; Foster City, CA 94404; (415) 570-7700; for $685.00. An Apple Macintosh version is also available.

Everybody's Planner is our low-priced favorite because it packs many features into a relatively inexpensive package. *Everybody's Planner* runs on IBM PC and fully compatible computers with 256K RAM, DOS 2.0 or higher, and an IBM, Epson, or Epson compatible dot matrix printer. The flowchart drawing routine requires a CGA Color Graphics Adapter and does not work with VGA, EGA, PGA, or Hercules graphics boards. A hard disk, mouse, and color monitor are optional.

The Apple version runs on Apple II+, IIe, IIc, and IIgs with 5.25 or 3.5 inch disks. *Everybody's Planner* is currently available from Abracadata; P.O. Box 2440; Eugene, Oregon 97402; (503) 342-3030 or (800) 451-4871; for $99.95. Demonstration disks for IBM compatible and Apple systems are available for $10.

Some Common Questions

People looking at the Project Planning Sheet for the first time ask a number of important questions. Let's see if we can answer yours as we go.

Where do the goals come from?

The goals can be either personal or professional. To be effective, they should be B.E.S.T. goals like those described in chapter 1. You can use the techniques described there to start defining your own goals.

How do you know what projects to work on?

That is an extraordinarily important question. You cannot fail to reach your goals if you pick the right projects and pursue them vigorously. Unfortunately, it's also a tough question to answer here because so much depends on who you are and what you want to accomplish. Here are some hints that may help you find your own answer.

For many people, friends or mentors can provide an answer, or at least get you pointed in the right direction. Talk to someone you trust, someone who has been successful and seems to understand the "ways of the world." You don't have to take their recommendations as gospel, but you can use them as a springboard on which to build your own plans.

Role models are another important source of information. Read biographies and autobiographies of the people you admire. Their projects and strategies may work for you, and you can always apply their ideas to your own situation.

Research is another key to finding appropriate projects. There is a staggering amount of information available in libraries of even moderate size. And most reference librarians will be delighted to help you get started. If your goals are financial, for example, there are countless sources of information that will tell you what career to pursue, what problems to anticipate, and how to "make it big."

Finally, your own creative imagination can point you in useful directions. This source of information is far more important than many people realize. Talking to friends and mentors, reading about your heroes, and conducting other research can tell you how people like you have accomplished goals similar to yours. Only your own creativity can help you find innovative ways to fulfill your goals.

Numerous books and seminars can introduce you to creative thinking techniques. There is even a new generation of computer programs designed to help stimulate creative thinking: the programs reviewed on this page and the next are among the best.

It has long been considered a mark of genius to find innovative solutions to common problems. Recent research has pointed to a surprising conclusion: everybody has the potential to be creative. Social conditioning, fear of rejection, rigid acceptance of popular assumptions, and lack of incubation time prevent most people from taking advantage of their natural creative abilities.

Becoming creative means learning to break free of these self-imposed restrictions. Brainstorming and other group activities help generate novel approaches to recurrent problems. These techniques are remarkably effective—under the proper circumstances. The hard part is finding groups of interested, open-minded people who have time to help.

Fortunately, there are a handful of computer programs that mimic the effects of friendly, supportive groups. The programs we have reviewed employ two approaches to stimulating creative problem solving. One approach asks carefully sequenced questions to help users clarify their own thinking. The other approach uses natural patterns of association and suggestion to prompt creative thinking. Our personal favorites in each of these categories are, respectively, the *Idea Generator Plus* and the *IDEAFISHER.*

The *Idea Generator Plus* uses techniques explained in *The Art of Creative Thinking*, by Gerard I. Nierenberg, a handy paperback book which is distributed with the program.

The *Idea Generator Plus* takes you through a gently structured problem solving process involving four steps. We say "gently structured" because you can break out of the routine at any time to record ideas in a separate idea screen and return to the structured problem solving process when you are ready.

Step one involves clarifying the problem. Interacting with the program, you generate a problem statement by describing the situation, listing your goals, and identifying other people involved.

The second step involves generating ideas. You work with any or all of seven techniques: reviewing similar situations, generating metaphors for the situation, looking at the problem from other perspectives, focusing on goals one at a time, reversing goals, attending to the people involved, and generalizing from ideas already generated.

The third step is evaluating ideas. You are guided through a step by step process: choosing ideas to evaluate, rating ideas by their impact on your goals, and looking at the ideas' costs, benefits, and effects on people. Because these steps can be time consuming, the *Idea Generator Plus* lets you save your work and take a break at any point.

The final step is preparing a report. You can print a complete summary of your problem solving session and even address memos to other people affected by the problem. In addition, and this is a very important feature, you can export your work to personal information managers like *Lotus Agenda, Think Tank,* and *Grandview,* or to a text file. A new release of the program also makes it possible to export files to *BestChoice3,* a decision-support program reviewed elsewhere.

The *IDEAFISHER* uses natural patterns of association to generate ideas. The program consists of four modules that help you define problems, explore associations, capitalize on alternate views, and record your ideas.

You begin in the QBank, a module consisting of more than 3,000 questions. Selecting questions that appear most relevant, you refine your understanding of the problem while your answers are stored in a second module, the Question Notepad. Once you have answered all selected questions, the Question Notepad is "filtered" so that key concepts are recorded in the Idea Notepad.

Working from concepts recorded in the Idea Notepad, you scan the Idea Bank, a collection of more than 60,000 words and phrases, for possible associations. Words and phrases can be moved in and out of the Idea Notepad with a few keystrokes, and you can record your own ideas as well.

A typical problem solving session may run several hours, but you can record your work, take a break, and restart the program at your convenience.

The *Idea Generator Plus* runs on IBM PC and fully compatible computers with 256K RAM, DOS 2.0 or higher and two floppy disk drives or a hard disk. *Idea Generator Plus* is currently available from Experience in Software; 2000 Hearst Avenue; Suite 202; Berkeley, California 94709-2176; (800) 678-7008 or (415) 644-0694; for $195.

IDEAFISHER runs on IBM PC and fully compatible computers with DOS 2.0 or higher, 512K RAM, and a hard disk. This is a large program and requires at least 7 megabytes of hard disk space. A printer and mouse are useful options, and an Apple Macintosh version is available. *IDEAFISHER* is currently available from Fisher Idea Systems; 18881 Von Karmen Ave; Irvine, CA 92715; (714) 474-8111; for $495.

How do you know what the finished product will look like?

Sometimes you are given a description of the finished project as part of an assignment. The report above is a good example because the instructor gave detailed instructions. At work and elsewhere you are likely to find many people who give explicit instructions and you can always ask for additional details.

There are also times when you need to create your own description. Think of it as creating your own assignment. Begin by summarizing everything you know about the task and then simply write out what you think you will produce as a result of the project. Don't worry about getting everything right—there will be time to revise and polish the description later. The important thing is to give yourself a target.

There are also times when you don't have a clear idea what the finished product will be. Some people prefer to plunge ahead and create a vision as they go—"on the fly," they say. You can follow their example if you wish, but we find another approach to be more productive.

Creating a vision should be the first step in your project planning sheet. And set a deadline for yourself. Understand that you may need to revise your view as you go along, but begin by working systematically to create the vision. You can use many of the techniques you would use to select a project. Talk to friends or mentors, look at examples from your role models, conduct some research, and put your creative imagination to work.

How do you divide a project into such neat steps?

Dividing a project into steps isn't difficult; it just takes a little time to work through the process. We like to begin with our vision of the finished product and work backwards. At each step ask yourself, "What do I need to complete this step?" Your answer will tell you what you need to do in the previous step. Your plan is complete when you get back to something you have already done or have.

Some people have difficulty dividing a project into steps because they are afraid of making a mistake. They are so anxious to get things right that they spend far too much time and effort at this step in the process. This fear is just another activity trap. We prefer to plunge ahead, knowing we can always revise our plan as we go.

You may fear that your plan will be set in concrete once you have finished the project planning sheet, but that is the case only when you need someone else's approval on the project. Sometimes it's your boss or a client, sometimes it's a coworker or teacher, and sometimes it's another member of your family. In a way, getting advance approval limits your freedom. But it also aids the learning process, because the person reviewing your work is often in a position to help you divide the project into steps. Rely on them and trust their judgment—as long as you are not asked to do anything illegal or unethical.

Who sets up the schedule of activities?

You do! Begin with the deadline and work backwards through each step. Some steps require more time than others and some are more important than others. Your time and abilities are the critical factors, and no one else is better prepared to schedule them than you are.

Of course you will make mistakes from time to time. That is part of the learning process. Forgive yourself when you make a mistake, and remember the lesson for the next project. And remember that a well defined project always includes a little extra time so you can recover from any errors.

What do you do when you fall behind?

The fact that you can fall behind is one of the real values of project management. Did that statement catch you off guard? Give us a minute to explain what we mean.

Time and again, we have seen people struggling to finish major projects at the last minute. Students regularly put in "all-nighters" before tests and due dates. We have also seen many professionals caught in the same bind. When we have been able to look back over their projects, we see that they have overlooked many early warning signs. A missed target date is a warning sign that ought to alert you to problems ahead.

There are several things you can do when you catch the warning signs early enough. First, make sure you are not caught in an activity trap. Is what you are doing really necessary? Can the end result be achieved without spending quite so much time on this step? Second, increase the resources committed to the project. Invest more of your time and energy, or look for someone else to help you. Third, revise your project plan. Look for other steps in the project that can be shortened. Finally, see if you can change the deadline. On personal projects, you set the deadlines. When other people are involved, you may have to negotiate for additional time. Changing the deadline may be the least attractive strategy, but it is also part of the learning process. You may set more realistic deadlines for yourself on the next project.

How many projects should I try to manage at a time?

There is no easy answer here because so much depends on who you are, how big the projects are, and what other responsibilities you carry. Our advice is to start small. Work with one or two at a time and gradually increase the number as you become more confident of your abilities. Eventually you will find a comfortable level of activity. And you will learn to anticipate the amount of work required in your projects and the kinds of resources you can devote to each.

If you are convinced that project management will help you organize your personal and professional life, feel free to make as many copies as you like of the sample Project Planning Sheet on the next page.

PROJECT PLANNING SHEET

GOAL:

FINISHED PRODUCT/DEADLINE:

PROJECT SUMMARY/TARGET DATES:

Whether you use paper and pencil or computer programs like *PS5*, project management is a powerful approach to organizing large tasks. However some jobs simply aren't suited to comprehensive project management.

For example, people in service roles are often responsible for doing lots of small tasks for others. Elaborate planning is inappropriate because each task is relatively simple and easy to complete. Although the tasks are small, the people performing them often feel swamped. Every day seems like a torrent of activity as participants try to keep a thousand balls in the air at once. The phrase, "up to their elbows in alligators," was invented to describe people in these jobs. Every organization has someone in this role and they all share a common feature: even though the individual tasks are small, they all play important roles in larger projects. You can't afford to let even one slip.

It's easy to spot the people who do this kind of job. Their desks are cluttered with to-do lists and reminders scribbled on Post-it Notes, desktop blotters, scraps of paper, rolodex cards, and backs of letters or memos. The greatest danger is that a critical note will be misplaced, resulting in a missed deadline.

If that sounds like your job, or if you know someone in a similar spot, you may be interested in a group of programs called Personal Information Managers (PIMs).

PIMs are designed to keep track of isolated pieces of information. They're just what the doctor ordered for people in high-stress service roles. *Instant Recall* is our favorite PIM.

Instant Recall is a memory resident program that you can call up at the touch of a single key. Using *Instant Recall*, you record information in any of four formats. The notes format is used for recording free-form information such as idea files, memos, lists, reports, and key facts. The tasks format is used for tracking and delegating responsibilities, establishing priorities, marking target dates, and providing advance warning of impending deadlines. The schedule format manages your calendar. It provides automatic conflict checking, a week-at-a-glance display, and open time display. Finally, the people format is used to record names, addresses, phone numbers, and notes.

Instant Recall runs on IBM PCs and fully compatible computers with DOS 3.0 or higher, 512K RAM, and a hard disk. You can also run *Instant Recall* in a nonmemory resident mode with DOS 2.1 and 720K disk space. It is easy to use and provides a number of other features: a pop-up timer, alarm messages, phone dialer, mouse support, password protection, and a clip board that lets you copy information from one application to another.

Instant Recall is currently available from Chronologic Corporation; 5151 North Oracle; Tuscson, Arizona 85794; (602) 293-3100; for $99. A version is also available for use on local area networks.

MANAGING YOUR WHOLE LIFE

Project Planning Sheets are the core of a powerful personal productivity management system. We would like to say that it is our system, but many of our clients have shared in the development process. Understanding how the system has grown will help you appreciate its power.

For some time we have encouraged our clients to keep their active Project Planning Sheets together in a single notebook. Keeping the sheets together makes it easy to do weekly reviews and plan the next steps of all the projects at once. Many clients following our advice have discovered that it is useful to keep other things in the same place with their project planning sheets. At first, there was a lot of variety in the things people added to the notebook. Some kept their to-do lists there. Others added weekly, monthly, and yearly calendars. A few found it useful to keep lists of personal and professional goals in the notebook, and some added phone numbers and addresses for people they needed to contact. Eventually, through trial and error, we developed a powerful personal productivity management system based on the experiences of our clients.

Our Personal Productivity Management System assembles all of the things you need to organize your personal and professional life in a single notebook. This system has the power to rival commercial systems costing several hundred dollars. It all fits in a single notebook, so you can take it with you and work on the run. And because it is personal, you can easily modify it to match your needs and interests. Of course, you can use the project planning sheets alone, but few people do once they see the whole system.

Let's start with an overview of the Personal Productivity Management System, and then we'll look at each of the parts in greater detail.

Overview: The Personal Productivity Management System

To the uninitiated, the Personal Productivity Management System looks like a simple notebook with five section dividers. If they looked no further, they would never recognize the power of the system because it's the stuff behind the dividers that is really important.

The major sections of a typical Personal Productivity Management System include (1) personal and professional goals, (2) Project Planning Sheets for active projects, (3) monthly calendars for the coming year, (4) day-by-day appointment sheets for the current month, and (5) a personal contacts list. These five sections and the notebook are the essential elements of the system. We'll take a minute or two to describe each.

If you like the idea of a personal productivity system but shy away from creating your own, you might want to look at some commercially available systems. Day-Timers, Inc., produces a broad line of personal time management systems and a brief review of their offerings shows what is available.

All Day-Timer systems include appointment books, daily to-do lists, reminders of coming deadlines, time logs, and expense records. These systems are available in four sizes with pages ranging from 2.75 × 5 inches for the smallest pocket edition to 8.5 × 11 inches for the desk edition. In addition, users may choose between permanently wire-bound and loose-leaf notebooks. We prefer the loose-leaf systems because we think their flexibility is a great advantage.

To a basic loose-leaf system you can add alphabetical, numerical, monthly, or blank tabs, as well as specialized pages. Some of the more useful pages include address/telephone number directories, frequent flyer logs, study notes, travel itineraries, meeting agenda planners, items to be discussed, action item lists, project fact sheets, performance planning forms, and delegation lists. You may also buy yearly project management sheets, full-year schedule pages, plastic business card holders, and monthly expense envelopes. Accessories include a desk-top stand, pen holders, and solar powered calculators.

Day-Timer systems are currently available from DAY-TIMERS, Inc.; One Day-Timer Plaza; Allentown, PA 18195; (215) 395-5889. Prices start at $10.95 for the smallest wire-bound version but you can spend $100 or more for a leather binder with specialized forms and accessories. Their attractive 90+ page catalog is a good introduction to some professional time management products.

The Notebook

Almost any sturdy 1.5 or 2 inch notebook will work fine. Small notebooks are convenient because they will fit in a purse, briefcase, or shirt pocket. We prefer full size notebooks because 8.5 by 11 inch paper can be three-hole punched and carried. That is an important consideration because it means you can slip letters, meeting agendas, and small reports in the notebook.

Simple, plastic or vinyl notebooks seldom cost more than a few dollars and work as well as more expensive notebooks. But many of our clients prefer elegant notebooks made of leather or exotic materials. They treat themselves to the expensive notebooks, they say, to announce that they "have arrived." More expensive notebooks add pockets for business cards, calculators, pens and pencils, checkbooks, and other accessories.

We think the expensive notebooks are nice but an inexpensive notebook will get the job done.

Dividers

Sets of sturdy dividers are available from almost every stationary store. We use two kinds. The first kind, with large tabs, can be used to divide the notebook into the major sections. The second kind, with preprinted tabs numbered 1 through 31, we use to separate days in the current month section.

Personal and Professional Goals.

The first section of the Personal Productivity Management System lists personal and professional goals. We use B.E.S.T. goals like those described in the last chapter. We include them in our notebooks because we like to review them every day.

Monthly Calendars

This is another piece we buy ready-made from the stationary store. Look for three-hole punched calendars with a full month on each 8.5 by 11 inch page.

There isn't much space to plan each day, but these calendars have enough room to note an appointment or two. They also let you plan major commitments a year or more in advance.

Current Month

The current month section is usually the largest section of the Personal Productivity Management System. Use the 1 through 31 tabs for individual days. You could use a commercial time management form for each day, but we prefer to design our own.

The important elements of each form will vary depending on what you need to accomplish. We use appointment schedules and to-do lists, so they figure prominently in the forms we use. We've also found it useful to leave some blank space on the bottom of the page for notes and comments. Other things that you might include are definitions of words you are learning to use, directions for a diet, money management tips, inspirational quotations, and sections for "pending business" with people you see regularly.

The following sample is taken from one of our books. Just think of it as an example: don't be limited by the form we use. Design your own to include everything you need to check on a daily basis. Once you are satisfied with your form, photocopy enough for the current month, three-hole punch them, and clip one in the notebook behind each of the 1 through 31 tabs.

	(day)	(month)	(date)

APPOINTMENTS	TO-DO
8:00AM	
9:00AM	
10:00AM	
11:00AM	
NOON	
1:00PM	
2:00PM	
3:00PM	
4:00PM	
5:00PM	
6:00PM	
7:00PM	

There is something else you may want to include in this section of the notebook. We used to spend lots of time filing agendas, memos, and other correspondence that we wanted to have with us in meetings or cross referenced with our to-do lists. Now we simply three-hole punch these items and slip them into our notebooks behind the appropriate dividers. We've found that if we keep everything together we spend a lot less time filing.

Contacts List

The final section of your Personal Productivity Management System should be your contacts list. Commercial forms are available, but we simply three-hole punch printouts of lists we keep on our personal computers. You may choose any form you like, but we rely on simple alphabetical lists of people with whom we work or need to talk to frequently. The lists aren't always complete, but the critical names, addresses, and phone numbers are all here.

The personal productivity management system described in this chapter is a useful way of organizing your work life. It makes it possible for you to work on the run because the system combines much of the information you need in a handy package. You may want to go a step further by coordinating files on your computer with information you can take along.

A standard word processor can be used to coordinate files from your computer with your personal productivity system. Simply create and store information regarding your personal projects, goals, schedule, and contacts in standard files created by your word processor. Edit them as you would any other file, and print updated reports periodically. Three-hold punch the printouts, clip them in the appropriate sections of your personal productivity system, and you are ready to run.

Using a word processor has a number of advantages. Most are quick and easy to use, you don't need to invest in new programs or hardware, and you don't need to learn any new techniques. In spite of these advantages, standard documents may not have the look and feel you want. If you want to do more than a word processor allows, here are a couple of options you may want to consider.

One of the new palmtop computers may be one of the most exciting options. These are fairly powerful computers that are small enough to fit in your pocket. They have built-in software for storing addresses and phone numbers, scheduling appointments, keeping track of expenses, and other tasks. Prices are falling, but you should expect to pay several hundred dollars for a full-functioned palmtop. If this strikes you as an attractive approach, see our review of the Atari *Portfolio* and the *POQET* elsewhere.

If you like the idea of a pocket-size computer but don't want to invest in a full-functioned one, you might consider a more limited unit. The *Personal Organizer* package with the *DataStor 8000* is a good example.

The pocket-size *DataStor* unit measures 3 × 5 ×.5 inches. It is a handy calculator with a convenient storage and retrieval function. When you turn it on, *DataStor 8000* places you in its directory mode and displays the first name stored in its file. Pressing the "linefeed" key brings up a single-line entry with that person's address or phone number. Pressing the "dir" key moves you to the next name on the list. A handy search routine lets you enter the first letter of any name so the display automatically moves to names which begin with that letter. *DataStor 8000* also displays time and date.

Because *DataStor* has a calculator-style keyboard, entering names and other information is tedious at best. Fortunately, the *Personal Organizer* package includes *PC Advantage*, software that allows you to enter and store information on your desktop computer. A cable and utility program permit you to transfer files to *DataStor 8000*. Most users will maintain and update files on their personal computers and simply "download" information to *DataStor 8000*.

The *Personal Organizer* includes an older release of Borland *Sidekick*, a program reviewed elsewhere. Versions are available for both IBM compatible PCs and Apple Macintoshes.

Then there are personal information managers, or PIMs, specialized programs designed to help professionals manage different kinds of information. Several include routines that allow you to print reports including project, contact, and to-do lists that you can carry with you in specialized binders. For additional details, see our reviews of *Instant Recall* and *who-what-when* elsewhere.

Finally, you might look at *Address Book Plus* by Power Up! This handy product is an all-in-one address book. The package has three components: a program for creating and maintaining address and telephone lists on your personal computer, precut paper for printouts, and a handy leather binder. Entries can be sorted by name, profession, date, company name, zip code, or comment line. You can import files from other programs and print mailing labels, rotary-file and index cards, and envelopes.

The *Personal Organizer* is currently available from Microlytics, Inc.; Two Tobey Village Office Park; Pittsford, New York, 14534; (800) 828-6293; for $84.95.

Address Book Plus is available for both IBM and fully compatible computers, and Macintosh computers. Printed lists can be sized for several popular commercial organizers as well as large (4.25 × 7 inch) and small (3.5 × 5.5 inch) pocket address books. *Address Book Plus* is currently available from Power Up!; 2929 Campus Drive; P.O. Box 7600; San Mateo, California 94403; (800) 851-2917 or (800) 223-1479 in California; for $119.95 (IBM and compatible version) and $129.95 (Macintosh version).

CONCLUSION

This chapter has introduced two key approaches that work well together: project management, and the personal productivity management system. If you want to take advantage of them right away, here's what you can do to get started.

First, assemble a notebook, dividers, and calendars. Clip them together and begin using the notebook as your central organizer.

Second, make copies of the daily schedule form for the rest of the month. Three-hold punch them, fill in the days and dates, and clip them in the notebook behind the appropriate dividers. Don't worry if our form doesn't quite fit your needs. You will find many ways to modify it over the next month. At the end of the month, you will be ready to create your own. Just don't let the design process keep you from acting now.

Third, make a list of your goals. This first draft will change as you gain experience, but right now it's important to get the list together. Three-hole punch this list and clip it in the notebook.

Fourth, make a list of your projects. Include everything you are working on, even if you haven't really gotten started. Once you have your list together, assign priorities. "A" projects are those you need to get done no matter what. We recommend you start with no more than five A projects. "B" projects are those you want to get to as soon as possible. These are important, but not as significant as the A projects. "C" projects are usually little more than rough ideas. They're the things you will explore when you have some time.

Fifth, develop project planning sheets for each of your A projects. Use the project plans to create to-do lists for each day of the month. Don't worry if you can't be as precise as you would like. You can revise and update your plans as you go along.

Finally, live with your productivity planner for a month. Write on it, change things around, add or remove pieces as you like. Every change you make should increase the system's value to you. Nothing is cast in concrete. Make the system personal and let it grow with you. At the end of the month, build your changes into the system for the next month.

SUGGESTED READINGS

Gilbreath, Robert D. *Winning At Project Management.* New York: John Wiley & Sons, 1986.

Kerzner, Harold. *Project Management for Executives.* New York: Van Nostrand Reinhold Company, 1982.

Levine, Harvey A. *Project Management Using Microcomputers.* Berkeley, California: Osborne McGraw-Hill, 1986.

Meredith, Jack R., and Samuel J. Mantel, Jr. *Project Management.* New York: John Wiley & Sons, 1985.

Whitmyer, Claude F. "Project and People Management With Tracking Software." *The Office,* February 1989, 24–25.

Chapter 3

HANDLING INTERRUPTIONS

COMMON PROBLEMS AND
TESTED SOLUTIONS

We first met Steve about a year ago when he enrolled in one of our productivity seminars. He stands out in our minds because he asked a really tough question—a question that mirrored the concerns of our audience and made us rethink some of the things we were teaching.

We were about two hours into the seminar when Steve raised his hand. We had already discussed keeping track of time, setting goals, and monitoring projects. In fact, we had covered much of the material you have read in the introduction and first two chapters of this book. Steve began by saying that he didn't want to offend us, but he had a question that couldn't wait. You can see for yourself what made his question so important.

"Just a minute," Steve said, "I think I understand what you are saying about goals and projects. In fact, I've got my goals written down and I've outlined the projects I'm working on. I can tell you exactly how I spend my time because I use a computer to help me keep track of billable hours. But, I still have a problem—really a bunch of problems.

"I've done everything you are talking about but I just can't get all my work done. I've got a to-do list a mile long and my desk is stacked two feet deep. Files, papers, and mail are everywhere. My secretary tries to help but it takes more time to show her what to do than to do it myself.

"I've tried setting aside time to get caught up, but I already work 75 hours a week. I don't think my family would let me get away with more.

"I've also tried closing my office door for a couple of hours each day. You can't imagine what a madhouse that creates: the phone starts ringing off the hook; people are lined up four deep waiting to ask me questions; and the minute I think I've got everything in order, my boss decides to call an emergency meeting.

"So here's my question: how do I control these interruptions so I can concentrate on my goals and projects?"

You can see why we think Steve's question is so important. If we lived in a private world, a world that we could control completely, goal setting and project planning would be enough. Unfortunately, we all live in a public world. Or, as some of our clients say, a *very public world*.

LIVING IN A PUBLIC WORLD

Realizing that we live in a public world is important because it points to one of the central problems in managing time. Other people think they have a right to a share of our time. Think about the number of people who make demands on you. They include friends, family members, customers, clients, employees, colleagues, and even bosses.

Many of these people have good reasons for believing they deserve a share of our time. Our jobs are often tied to the public world. If you are a manager, the most important part of your job requires dealing with a public: your coworkers. In fact, studies indicate that many senior managers spend as much as 85% of their time being interrupted.

We could make the same point about many other occupations. Everyone in personal and professional services has a job that invites interruptions. Careers in education and sales also open the door for interruptions. In fact, our economy is moving in ways that create more and more jobs that involve working with—and being interrupted by—other people.

In the last few years, a number of products have been promoted as executive assistants. They promise to make life easier by scheduling appointments, managing people, and tracking projects. Unfortunately, few of these programs really match the way we've seen executives work.

However we have found one that does match the way we work and the way we think most professionals work. *who-what-when* is an extraordinary program that has replaced all of the other time and project management systems we have used.

Using *who-what-when*, you define projects, schedule appointments, list to-do items, and update your contacts list by typing information into a personal daily calendar. *who-what-when* is smart enough to simplify the process for you in a number of ways. For example, time entered as "1p" automatically becomes "1:00 P.M." Phone numbers entered as ten digits are automatically formatted to show area codes, prefixes, and line numbers. Dates can be entered in three ways: typing in six digits, highlighting a day on the built-in calendar, or with a special shorthand. Using the shorthand approach, +10 means ten days from now. A memo function lets you attach more detailed information to any entry.

who-what-when entries can be displayed in any of three categories. The "who" view lets you see phone lists, mailing addresses, and projects or tasks assigned to each person.

The "what" view focuses on projects and automatically builds Gantt Charts from daily calendar entries. You can also "zoom" in on particular projects to look at specific task details.

Finally, the "when" view prepares daily schedules and to-do lists. Schedules for several people can be coordinated and a special Meeting Maker identifies times when everyone in any group you select is available for a meeting.

The thing that makes *who-what-when* really special is the extent to which these three views are integrated. The who view lets you see everything you are doing with another person, the what view shows the status of your projects, and the when view displays your schedule for the day. Whenever you schedule an appointment with a new person, *who-what-when* recognizes that this person isn't in your contacts list and prompts you to input the needed information. That's important for first-time users because you don't have to set aside a great deal of time to enter information from your old system. *who-what-when* prompts you for information as you work, so you can begin using it to schedule your life as soon as you have it installed on your computer.

Because the three views are fully integrated, project deadlines, tasks, and milestones are automatically built into your personal calendar. If you don't complete an item on the day scheduled, *who-what-when* carries it over to the next day. The program will continue reminding you about the task until you mark it completed.

Management reports summarizing projects, activities, personal contacts, and detailed daily calendars can be printed by day, week, or month. Since you may not always be able to get to your PC, *who-what-when* prints schedules, project summaries, and contact lists in sizes compatible with popular personal organizers so you can take them with you wherever you go.

who-what-when runs on IBM PCs and fully compatible computers with 512K RAM, DOS 2.1 or higher, and a hard disk. *who-what-when* is currently available from Chronos Software Inc.; 555 DeHaro Street; Suite 240; San Francisco, CA 94107; (800) 777-7907 or (415) 626-4244; for $295. A LAN (local area network) version called *Enterprise* serving up to six people sells for $695.

There are many people away from work who also have good reason to believe they can interrupt us at their pleasure. Friends and family members have very legitimate claims on our time and attention. Representatives of social service agencies, public organizations, and charitable institutions may also have good claims on us. And it is fair to say that we sometimes interrupt ourselves. Few of us have the capacity to work without interruption. Body and spirit combine at times to pull us away from our tasks. You ignore their calls at your own peril.

Every day, we are bombarded by ingenious new interruptions: letters, newspapers, magazines, journals, memos, telephones, television programs, electronic messages . . . the list goes on and on. And just when we think we have figured out how to control these intrusions, some damn fool calls a meeting.

ↄↄↄ

The need to keep up with new ideas and master new skills poses an ongoing challenge, particularly for professionals with tight schedules. While classic works continue to have relevance, thousands of new books and countless articles are published every year. New seminars are introduced every day. Few professionals have time to read even a fraction of the material produced. It is frequently impossible to get away to a seminar.

Many professionals have discovered that they can use tape recordings to ease demands on their time. They listen to the tapes while driving, exercising, or engaging in routine activities.

One-tape condensations of some books are available at many bookstores for around $10. More comprehensive programs are available from Nightingale Conant Corporation, a leading supplier of tape-recorded programs.

Recent Nightingale Conant releases include *Head First*, by Norman Cousins; *$ix Figure Selling*, by Tony Alessandra, Phil Wexler, and Rick Barrera; *Thriving on Chaos* and *The New Masters of Excellence*, by Tom Peters; and *How to Win Customers and Keep Them for Life*, by Michael LeBoeuf. Classic programs include *Lead the Field*, by Earl Nightingale; *Think and Grow Rich*, by Napolean Hill; and *Psycho-Cybernetics*, by Maxwell Maltz.

Prices vary but most are around $60 for conveniently packaged programs with six audio cassettes. Videotaped programs are also available at noticeably higher prices. For additional information, write Nightingale-Conant Corporation; 7300 North Lehigh Avenue; Chicago, Illinois 60648; (800) 525-9000.

CREATING BALANCE IN YOUR LIFE

Living in a public world can be a nuisance—there is no doubt about that. And yet we know of no one who prefers complete isolation. There may be a few hermits in the world, but the fact that we haven't met them tells you something about them, and us!

The simple fact is that we live in a public world. It's also a fact that we can have as much private time as we like—we could all become hermits—if we are willing to accept the consequences. It's up to each of us to find our own comfortable balance.

There are several tests designed to help people find the balance with which they are comfortable. Many of these tests distinguish between introverts, people who need lots of private time, and extroverts, people who need lots of public time.

⚒ ⚒ ⚒ ⚒

If you have never taken one of these tests, you may want to check your local library for a copy of *Please Understand Me*, by David Keirsey and Marilyn Bates (Del Mar, California: Prometheus Nemesis Book Company, 1984). Chapter One includes a self-scoring test that will help you find your centering point on introversion-extraversion and on three other dimensions. The rest of the book is a thoughtful discussion of the way personal differences affect our daily lives.

These tests are valuable, but we prefer our own checklist. Take a minute to answer each of the following questions.

Do you feel guilty because you are spending too much time with family and friends?

Do you feel tired or stressed because things are not getting done?

Are you under pressure at work because of missed deadlines?

Are you starting to feel overwhelmed by clutter at home and at work?

Do you feel like you are constantly jumping from one thing to another?

If you answered yes to three or more questions, there is a good chance that you need more private time. We aren't suggesting that you ignore people and events around you, but it is pretty clear that you are in danger of being overwhelmed by the public world. To do the things you want, and to protect yourself from stress, you need to find some ways of dealing with intrusions.

HANDLING INTRUSIONS

We offer this chapter to you as an elaborate "tips" list. In the following pages you will find some of the ways people have dealt with intrusions in their lives. We've learned many of these tips from people in our seminars, and we have practiced them ourselves.

Some may appear silly or unworkable. Don't be upset if you don't like everything you read. Each of us has his/her own personal style. Things that work for one may not work for others. Things that solve problems for one person may annoy others or create even greater problems for still others.

So read this chapter selectively. Try the things that make sense to you; disregard the things that just don't seem practical. But we encourage you to reread this chapter from time to time. You may find use later for some things that seem irrelevant now, and there may be times when you will need to find new ways of dealing with intrusions in your life.

Many older personal computers can do only one thing at a time. This can create quite a problem when you are interrupted in the midst of one project and want to use your computer for something else, even for a moment.

For example, suppose you need to look up a phone number in your data base while you are writing a report with a word processor. This simple task requires you to save your report, exit the word processor, change directories to the one containing your data base, start your data base, load the appropriate data, look up the phone number, save the data base, exit the data base program, change directories to the one containing your word processor, restart your word processor, reload your report, and resume writing. That is quite a nuisance, and of course it slows you down considerably.

Fortunately, there are programs designed to avoid this problem: they're called terminate-stay-resident programs. *Sidekick Plus* is a leader in this field. A brief review of its features will show you how powerful it is.

Sidekick Plus is actually seven programs in one:

a file manager for locating files and copying files from one disk or directory to another,

a writer that records information in as many as nine notepads, a sophisticated outliner,

a phonebook that can automatically dial numbers if your computer is equipped with a modem,

a time planner with calendar, appointment book, and alarms to remind you of appointments,

a calculator that mimics functions of business, scientific, programmer, and formula calculators, and

a clipboard that you can use to transfer information from one program to another.

When you turn on your computer, you load *Sidekick Plus* before you load the program you plan to use. You can use a special file (called an autoexec batch file) to load *Sidekick Plus* so you don't even have to worry about the process. Once loaded, *Sidekick Plus* stays hidden in your computer until you need it. Most other programs such as word processors, spreadsheets, and data bases work normally with *Sidekick Plus* hidden behind them because there is enough memory for both.

Whenever you want to use *Sidekick Plus,* you press a special combination of keys to freeze the program you are using and call up *Sidekick Plus.* Once you have called up *Sidekick Plus,* you can use as many of its programs as you like. When you are done, a press of the escape key returns you to the frozen program at the exact spot where you interrupted it. *Sidekick Plus* then returns to hiding until you need it again.

Sidekick Plus runs on IBM PC and fully compatible computers with DOS 2.0 or higher, 384K RAM, and a hard disk. *Sidekick Plus* is currently available from Borland International; 1800 Green Hills Road; Post Office Box 660001; Scotts Valley, CA 95067-0001; (800) 331-0877; for $199.95.

Make Planning Part of Your Routine

We start with this piece of advice because we think it is the most important. Time and again, we've met people who complained about not getting anything done. We usually respond by asking them a single question: How do you plan your days? The blank stare we often get in response tells us we've uncovered the cause.

Many tasks and activities are like rabbits—they expand to fill available space. Unless you have formed a plan for using your time, you are likely to spend time on the first thing that catches your attention. But that activity may not be the most productive way to spend your time. That's why we're such strong advocates of planning.

In fact, we encourage people to set up four planning cycles. The longest planning cycle is one year. We think people ought to spend some time every year reviewing their goals and sketching a general plan for the coming year. Of course, yearly plans can't be as precise as you might like, but they can form a general sense of direction.

Your yearly plan should include a review of your major goals. Some may drop off the list because you've already accomplished them. Some may be less relevant than previously, others will become more important, and new goals may be added to the list.

In addition to reviewing your goals, take some time to review the projects on which you are working. Compare your progress to your original plan to see if you are on target. If you've fallen behind, try to formulate strategies for catching up. If you're ahead of schedule, see how you can take advantage of that.

While yearly plans are necessarily imprecise, monthly plans can be relatively exacting. We like to use the last Sunday of each month to make our plans for the next month. Monthly plans are similar to yearly ones, but they are much more exact. Review each project, noting those that are ahead of schedule, on target, and falling behind. This is also the best time to implement changes in your general plan. If you are ahead of schedule, give yourself an extra day off. But if you've fallen behind, plan to use an extra day or two to catch up—even if it means giving up a holiday.

Weekly plans are more precise still. We are in the habit of taking some time every Sunday to plan for the week ahead. We like to start each week knowing exactly what we need to accomplish. We decide how much time to spend on each project and schedule that time around other events and activities.

The final planning cycle is the most precise. It is also the easiest. Every evening, we take a few minutes to review our schedule for the next day. At this stage, appointments and other activities can be scheduled precisely. Free time can be allocated, and specific tasks planned with care.

AIM TO LEAD A BALANCED LIFE

To us, balance is an essential element. In fact, we began working on time management when we noticed that most books on the subject seemed interested only in professional applications.

As you saw in the introduction, we like to think of dividing our activities into six major categories:

- personal maintenance: sleeping, eating, showering, shaving

- self-development: exercise, professional reading, studying

- financial: earning income, time on the job or in free-lance work

- social activities: time with family and friends

- community service: voluntary work helping others, not for pay

- relaxation: resting, pleasure reading, sitting in the sun

We also add an "other" category because everyone has unique needs and interests.

The point is that all of these kinds of activity are important. You ought to plan some time for each of them in your daily routine. Of course everyone has his or her own sense of balance and you may need far more activity in one category than in the others. That's OK, that's what it means to be an individual. However, neglecting any of these categories can lead to trouble. Failing to exercise can lead to physical problems, just as failing to develop yourself mentally can lead to emotional problems.

Set Reasonable Expectations

We all do a lot of things by habit. Many of our habits were set when we were very young—some by the time we were six years old. Changing unproductive habits is one of the purposes of studying time management, but you need to set reasonable expectations for yourself along the way.

People can make dramatic changes in their behavior, but it often takes time. For example, if you normally sleep nine hours a day, you may be able to cut back to four or five—if you give yourself enough time. However, if you try to make the transition overnight—you are bound to be disappointed. You will probably be able to force yourself to run on four hours a night for a while, but then your body will rebel and you will be right back where you started, or worse.

Changing any habit is a lot like changing our sleep habits. We can make enormous changes if we give ourselves enough time. The rule of thumb is to *make a consistent effort over time.* Reduce sleep by cutting back fifteen minutes a night every week or two. Change other habits the same way. Don't build frustration by trying to do too much too fast.

Schedule Time for Personal Activities

We think of personal activities as all of the things you do for yourself, often just to make yourself feel good. Exercise, relaxation, listening to a symphony, attending a play, and playing golf are all examples of personal activities. They can even be as simple as shining your shoes.

We think you ought to build them into your schedule just so you don't forget to do them. Unfortunately, personal activities are likely to be overlooked in times of crisis and pressure. But these are the times when you most need to take time out for yourself.

In our workshops, we recommend that people set aside a minimum of 30 minutes a day just for themselves. Some people have good reasons for arguing with us, but we usually win our point: you need time for yourself just to keep running at your normal pace. If you don't schedule it, you may forget and that can lead to trouble.

Schedule Time for Things You Least Like

This recommendation may surprise you. "Why in the world," you may ask, "should I set aside time for things I don't like doing?" Our answer is that there is a lot of stuff that needs doing, stuff that piles up until you are forced to deal with it. Examples include stacks of junk mail in your in box, dirty clothes in the hamper, shirts waiting to go to the laundry, routine filing, monthly or other bills, and so forth.

All this "stuff" includes things you don't like to do, but which need to be done eventually. If you don't set aside time for them, they won't get done until you hit a crisis and can't avoid them. Then you are forced to throw yourself headlong into the task until you are past the immediate problem.

We think it is much easier to do a little at a time. Perhaps just 20 minutes a day. We suggest 20 minutes because you can get a lot done in that time, and it helps to know that it will be over soon. One of our clients told us that you "can survive anything for 20 minutes because you know it's almost over." We don't want to take her too literally, but the point is a good one.

Schedule Time for Things You Like Most

This recommendation is the companion to the one above it. Just as it's important to get through the "stuff," it's important to set aside time for the things you enjoy. You can think of this time as a reward for all your hard work.

There's also another reason for setting aside time for the things you like. We've all seen people under pressure who forego doing the things they like. These people get an awful lot done for a while, but that while doesn't go on for ever. They neglect time for themselves until eventually they reach their breaking point. But by then they may not be in control and may be forced to take time away at just the wrong moment.

Being forced to take time off at the wrong time is like taking two steps backwards for every one forward. It is much better to avoid that problem by planning regular opportunities to do things you like.

Remember Your A B Cs

Everybody we know uses a to-do list. In fact, these lists are so common that we don't even make a big point of them. However, there is one particular feature that needs to be emphasized.

A simple to-do list is better than none—unless it gets overwhelmingly long. When a list gets so long that you don't know where to start, you may get so frustrated that you throw the list away, hoping there was nothing "really important" on it, and start over. We sympathize with the frustration, but think there is a better way.

We use the phrase "A B Cs" to remind ourselves that it is important to rank the jobs on our to-do lists. Every morning we begin by reviewing the to-do list, rating the importance of each job. An "A" is a task that absolutely must get done today, no matter what else comes up. A "B" is something that would be nice to do if possible. Bs are important, but we won't lose sleep if we don't get them done. Finally, "C"s are things that we will get around to eventually. Cs may be important, but not crucial, at least not yet. And keep in mind that today's B may be an A tomorrow, while today's C may be a B tomorrow and an A the next day.

The A B Cs is a useful way to break down your list. Begin every day by working on your As and you will be happier and more productive.

Use a Deadline List

A deadline list is like a to-do list but it is organized a little differently. Instead of organizing tasks by A B Cs, a deadline list organizes tasks by their deadlines, the dates and times when they must be finished.

Although we use to-do lists most of the time, we shift to deadline lists when we face a lot of deadlines. We find the deadline list is best in high pressure situations where we really need to "keep on top of things." We typically use deadline lists for a week or so at a time, and then shift back to to-do lists when the pressure is off. You may want to try the same strategy.

Limit Paper Handling

We all get hit with so much paper every day that it is easy to let things slip. Just look at the number of things that accumulate in your in box when you are away from your office for a day or two. You are likely to find a mixture of letters, memos, reports, journals, magazines, junk mail, and trade announcements.

Most organizations live and breathe by paper and that's OK as long as things are flowing smoothly. We may not like the amount of time required to get through all of it, but most of us realize that it's just part of the job. However, some pieces of paper get "hung up" in the system. These are usually things we aren't quite sure what to do with. Sometimes there are letters we don't know how to answer, or even if we want to answer. There may also be articles or reports that we may want to read "someday," and reports that we may save "just in case."

Even a few pieces hung in the system can cause enormous backlogs because we end up going over them again and again. We weren't sure what to do with it yesterday so it went back in the in box. We haven't made up our minds today so it goes back in the in box again. After a while, your in box can become an oversized and unorganized file of uncertainty and anxiety.

Here's how you get out of the cycle. Every time you handle a piece of paper you don't know what to do with, tear off one corner. When all four corners are gone, throw it away. That recommendation may make you nervous and you may get caught "with your pants down" occasionally, but you will be able to get things moving again much faster without all that stuff accumulating in your in box.

Personal schedulers like *who-what-when* and desktop organizers like *Sidekick Plus*, reviewed elsewhere, are powerful additions to a computer user's software collection. However, many users don't need the power of a dedicated personal scheduler but still want more than a simple desktop organizer.

If you are in that in-between group, you may want to consider a program that handles some scheduling tasks, provides a desktop organizer, and helps to control your PC itself. If that sounds attractive, consider *PCTools Deluxe*, version 6.

PCTools Deluxe combines a personal scheduler with utility programs that help you manage your personal computer. The desktop manager includes notepads with a spelling checker, an appointment scheduler, a pop-up calculator, and a cut-and-paste feature that lets you move information from one application to another. Additional features include support for fax boards and electronic mail, and a dBASE compatible data base.

Computer management features include routines to make backup copies of files, special programs to recover data from damaged disks, and a "shell" that makes it easier to use DOS commands and locate misplaced files.

PCTools Deluxe, version 6 is designed to work with IBM PC, XT, AT and fully compatible computers and with all IBM PS/2 models. It requires 512 K RAM, DOS version 3.0 or higher, and at least one disk drive. *PCTools Deluxe* is currently available from Central Point Software, Inc.; 15220 N.W. Greenbrier Parkway, Suite 200; Beaverton, Oregon 97006; (503) 690-8090; for $149.

Ask Lakein's Question

Alan Lakein's book, *How to Get Control of Your Time and Your Life,* is one of our all-time favorite books on time management. The whole book is great, but one specific piece of advice stands out.

Whenever you have a free moment, whether you are waiting for an appointment, stuck in traffic, or just sitting at your desk, ask yourself Lakein's question: "what is the best use of my time right now?"

There is no simple right or wrong answer. "Taking a minute to relax" is as good an answer as "finishing the Johnson report." The important thing is that just asking the question puts you in control. Not asking the question leaves you at the mercy of whatever is happening around you.

Set Time Limits

This may be one of our more controversial recommendations; we know several people who argue vigorously against it. However, we find it useful more often than not.

We often see people let their projects take control of them. They start with a task and stick with it until finished. Then they move on to the next one. That's not bad in most cases, but it seems to us that some projects will take as much time as you let them. That is, these tasks expand to fill the time available and you find yourself spending seemingly endless amounts of time on them.

We think you can get out of that cycle by setting a time limit. Before you begin, decide how much time you will spend on the project. Set a limit and stick with it. Many tasks can be finished far more rapidly than you anticipate. Just setting a limit puts you in control.

Use a Timer

This recommendation works hand in hand with the last one. Once you get in the habit of setting time limits, you need a way of sticking to them. You could keep an eye on the clock or listen to the radio for time signals, but either of these tactics distracts you. We prefer the best time management tool you can buy for under $10—a simple countdown timer.

Ours came from Radio Shack, but they must be available elsewhere. We keep them on our desks. You can set the timer to count down from as much as 100 minutes or as little as 30 seconds. We set it when we start a timed task, knowing that the soft beep-beep-beep will alert us when it's time to move on. When we want to make sure we're on time for an appointment, we set it five minutes early so we can get everything wrapped up before we move on.

Time is money, especially for professionals who bill clients on an hourly or project basis. Accountants, architects, construction managers, consultants, financial planners, graphic designers, interior designers, lawyers, nurses, and psychologists are just a few of the professionals who may need to keep track of their hours serving clients.

Keeping track of the time isn't very complicated. You just keep a list of hours working for each client. However, it can be a real aggravation when you are working on several projects for different clients at the same time. You may be working on a project for one client when you get a call from another who needs help with two projects, and so on. Many professionals simply make their best guess when it comes to allocating time in these situations.

Fortunately, a new generation of programs has made sophisticated time tracking and billing procedures available to anyone with a personal computer. *Timeslips III* is a good example of its type. This is a remarkably powerful program, but a brief review of its features will show you what you can expect.

Timeslips III has two parts. The first part, *TSTimer*, is used to keep track of your time as you work. Most people set it up as a terminate-stay-resident program, just like *Sidekick Plus* described earlier.

TSTimer uses client records you create and includes a stopwatch to measure your time on each project. Let's look at a typical professional's day to show you how it works.

For example, let's say you begin your day writing a report for one client, Carol Smith. Start by calling up your record for Carol Smith and turning on the stopwatch. *TSTimer* will continue to accumulate time on Carol Smith's account until you tell it to stop. You may switch to your word processor and continue working until lunch. However, you may be interrupted by calls and other activities. For example, another client, Bob Howard, may stop in to discuss a project with which he needs help. As Bob walks in, simply call up his record and turn on the stopwatch. This automatically stops accumulating time on Carol Smith's account and begins charging it to Bob Howard. When Bob leaves, you may go back to work on Carol's report, break for lunch, or work on another project for another client. *Timeslips III* will track your time automatically as long as you remember to shift the stopwatch. Don't worry if you occasionally forget, because you can always go back and edit your records.

The second part of *Timeslips III* is *TSReport*. Its job is to collect all of the data created by *TSTimer* and turn it into useful information. Many professionals run *TSReports* once a month, but you can use any billing cycle you like. When you run it, *TSReports* examines all of the records generated by *TSTimer* and analyzes time spent on each client and project. Using this information, you can create a detailed report for yourself, analyze your own time usage, and prepare bills for clients. *TSReports* lets you choose the billing format you like, and reviews bills on screen before printing.

Timeslips III is a sophisticated program; this review has merely touched on some of its features. The first three chapters of the owner's manual provide a useful overview, but readers may feel that there are some loose ends. It may take several hours of study to overcome this feeling, but we think most professionals will find it time well spent.

Timeslips III runs on IBM PC and fully compatible computers with 448K RAM, DOS 2.1 or higher, and a hard disk. The Apple Macintosh version requires a Mac Plus, SE, II, IIx, or 512KE with at least 1MB RAM; System 4.2 and Finder 6.0 or later; two 800K floppy drives or an 800K floppy drive and hard disk. *Timeslips III* is currently available from Timeslips Corporation; 229 Western Ave.; Essex, MA 01929; (508) 768-6100; for $299.95.

Delegate Whatever You Can

Delegation is so important that we've devoted a whole chapter to it. But we wanted to make sure you keep it in mind in this context as well.

Whenever you find yourself getting overwhelmed with work, look at the people around you. If they are all working hard too, you are probably doing pretty well. But if the people who work for you have time to goof off while you are killing yourself, you may want to look at the way you assign work.

The handy rule of thumb is *delegate as much as you can; never do something you can assign to someone else.* That is a pretty sweeping rule and there are a number of exceptions, but we'll discuss them in the next chapter.

Group Tiny Tasks

There are times when all of us confront what we call "tiny tasks." We don't use the word "tiny" to imply that these tasks are unimportant. On the contrary, some of them are very important. But they are often so small that none of them would take much time by themselves. The problem is that we are all inclined to let them slip until we find ourselves confronted with an overwhelming list of "small stuff."

We deal with this problem by grouping or clustering tiny tasks. We look to see what they have in common and then do a bunch of them at once. Let's look at a couple of examples to show you what we mean.

Sometimes several tasks involve the same location. It makes sense to cluster errands that all involve driving to the same area or location. Other tasks may have the same people in common. Rather than running next door to see your neighbor every time you think of something interesting to discuss, you might wait until you have several items to bring up. Other tasks have the same activity in common. You might pay all of your bills once a week or set aside one day a month for writing letters.

We could add several more examples but the principle should be clear: you can get through lots of tiny tasks at once by grouping them logically. Combine items that can be "piggybacked" and done all at once.

Learn to Say "No!"

Saying "No" is never easy, especially when a friend requests a favor. However all of us reach that point where one more task is too much. It becomes the proverbial straw that broke the camel's back. This is when you have to say "No," politely but firmly.

The hard part is saying "No" in a way that preserves your relationship with the other person. Next time you find yourself in this spot, try something like the following.

"I understand how important this is to you and I'd really like to help. I'm just so busy that I couldn't give it the time it deserves. Have you asked Steve for help?"

Nothing will work all the time, but this response is the best we've seen. It shows you are sensitive to the other person and gives them an alternative while protecting your time—and your sanity.

Schedule for Predictable Interruptions

Interruptions are part of every job. Some studies say that managers spend as much as 85 percent of their time being interrupted. We haven't seen any studies on the subject of interruptions off the job, but we guess that they are as frequent as they are at work.

Much as we would like to avoid them, interruptions are a constant fact for most of us and we need to include this fact in our planning. Scheduling for interruptions has two elements.

First, if you know you are going to be interrupted several times during a typical day, don't plan your days as if there were no interruptions. An eight-hour work day may only have two or three hours of uninterrupted working time. Schedule your projects accordingly.

Second, you can control some interruptions by scheduling time for them. For example, if you have one or two subordinates who feel the need to check with you before making decisions, build in time every day to meet with them. A brief meeting in the morning or afternoon can give you a chance to deal with several items at once so you won't be interrupted later.

We often think of visits, meetings, phone calls, letters, and memos as interruptions. For most of us, they are interruptions because they interfere with the orderly conduct of our business, whatever it may be.

However, for many people, visits, meetings, phone calls, and memos are vital to their business. Salespeople are good examples because their business literally lives and dies on the strength of their contacts with customers. Bright salespeople seldom treat communications from customers as interruptions. We can all benefit from their example.

Salespeople are not unique in this regard: almost everyone is dependent on contact with others. Customers, clients, colleagues, partners, investors, or even casual acquaintances are important to everyone. Managing contact with these people is less a matter of avoiding interruptions than of scheduling contacts in an orderly way. Moreover, you need to make sure that you don't miss appointments, fail to make good on promises, or overlook important events.

You can keep track of contacts with paper and pencil systems, but revising and updating files can take an enormous amount of time. And cross-referencing your datebook with clients' requests can be difficult.

Fortunately, there are a number of computer programs designed to take the drudgery out of managing contacts with customers, clients, and other important people in your life.

ACT! by Contact Software International is one of the most popular products of this type. *ACT!* combines an organizer, record keeper, phone directory, notebook, appointment calendar, calculator, letter writer, label maker, report generator, sales and lead tracker, and tickler in one, easy to use package.

When you start the program, *ACT!* automatically loads profiles of people you are tracking. This data base is the heart of the system, and *ACT!* makes it easy to add, delete, or revise entries.

ACT! is far more than a simple data base. Menu-driven commands make it easy to do almost everything you need to manage contacts with people in the data base. You can call (*ACT!* will even dial the phone if your computer is equipped with a modem), write a personal letter or memo, send a form letter, schedule appointments and meetings, review recent contacts, and create a to-do list. *ACT!* will prepare a daily schedule of contacts for you and even set alarms so you don't overlook appointments or other obligations.

For all this power, *ACT!* is surprisingly easy to use. The well-written manual is easy to follow, while the demonstration program and video introduction make learning to use the program a snap.

ACT! runs on IBM PC and fully compatible computers with 460K RAM, DOS 2.0 or higher, and a hard disk or two 720K disk drives. A new version on credit-card-size ROM cards has been released for the *Poqet* palmtop computer. *ACT!* is currently available from Contact Software International, Inc.; 1625 W. Crosby Rd., #132; Carrollton, TX 75006; (214) 418-1866; for $395. Demonstration software and video introduction are available for $15.

Limit Conversations and Informal Meetings

"Have you got a minute?" should top most professionals' lists of threatening phrases. The person who asks the question usually feels an urgent need to speak with you and often needs more than a minute. It's difficult to say "no" because there might be a real need to speak to you, but saying "yes" opens the door to limitless interruptions.

Here's how we have learned to get out of this bind. When someone asks us if we "have a minute," we answer by saying something like "Yes, but just barely.

Is two minutes enough or would you like to make an appointment to see me later?"

The nice thing about this answer is that it puts responsibility back where it belongs—with the other person. If they can explain what they need in two minutes, good. If not, make arrangements to see them later. And, in cases of real emergency, you get the information you need to evaluate the situation.

Here are some other tricks you can use to control this kind of interruption.

• Remain standing so the other person knows you can't stay long.

• Set a timer to limit the length of the conversation.

• Have your secretary buzz you when your next appointment arrives.

• Interrupt the other person when you have heard enough to make a judgment and find another time to deal with the matter—preferably at a regularly scheduled meeting.

Show Others How to Use Your Time

People who interrupt you most frequently may not realize that it causes you a problem. And they may not realize they have any alternatives. The chapter on delegation introduces several ways for managing this problem, but there are a few things you can begin to do immediately.

First, set a time limit for casual interruptions, and stick with it. People have a surprising knack for getting to the point when they know the clock is running.

Second, make sure people understand your priorities. Each time they bring an item to you, use it as an opportunity to show them whether the matter is or is not important enough to warrant future interruptions.

Finally, introduce them to the "folder" technique. The folder technique is a simple way of clustering interruptions. Make a separate folder for each of the people you work with. Whenever you have something to discuss with them, make a note and drop it in the appropriate folder. When the person comes in to see you for any reason, answer their questions and then pull your folder and run through all the items you want to discuss with them. It won't take long for them to get the idea and create their own set of folders.

Meditate, Relax, Recharge Your Batteries

This tactic is so simple we almost didn't include it. Then we realized that some people have never tried it.

Whenever you feel overwhelmed, take ten minutes for yourself. Close your door, loosen your collar, lean back, and close your eyes for a few minutes. There are even audio tapes designed to help you slip into a more relaxed state of mind for a brief period. If you are worried about dozing off, set a timer to bring you back to the real world.

If you've never tried this, you will be amazed at how much good a few minutes of relaxation can do. You will return to work with renewed vigor and energy, and probably have a clearer sense of what needs to be done.

Continue Learning About Time Management

You have already taken a big step by reading this book. You can continue to grow by attending seminars and workshops, reading some of the suggested readings following each chapter of this book, and experimenting with some of the products reviewed in this book and elsewhere.

Continuous learning is particularly important because your responsibilities continue to change. Techniques that once worked will become less effective. Old habits may become self-limiting, and new technologies may be developed. Simply reviewing your patterns from time to time will also help you stay on top of things.

Add Fifteen Minutes to Your Day

Although our bodies need a minimum amount of sleep, most of us get far more than we need. You can add to your day by getting up fifteen minutes earlier or staying up fifteen minutes later than normal. Your body probably won't know the difference, or will get used to the new routine quickly, but fifteen minutes a day adds up to over 90 hours of potentially productive time every year.

Save No-Brain Work for Late Evenings

Fatigue catches up with everybody in the late evenings. This is an ideal time for what we call "no-brainers," simple repetitive tasks that have to be done but which don't require much concentration. Shining shoes, sorting junk mail, cleaning the kitchen, you name it. Whatever needs to be done but doesn't require serious thought is an ideal candidate for late night work.

Break Out of Activity Traps

Activity traps are ongoing activities that never seem to come to an end. We don't even know where they all come from, but we have seen several common types. Some activity traps begin as purposeful activities but become habits that stay with us long after their reasons have ceased to exist. Other activity traps are projects that never seem to end, usually because we haven't decided what the conclusion will be. And still other activity traps are rituals established by other people. They were fun activities to share when they started, but now are just things we do because we're expected to.

You can probably add several categories to our list. The important thing is finding ways to escape from the traps. Here are some suggestions.

First, set a time limit for repetitive activities. You may find that they can be done in less time than you realized. In an extreme case, you may even find that limiting your time gives you an excuse for stopping altogether.

Second, set a goal. Determine how much or how many times a thing has to be done. Simply stop when you have reached your goal.

Finally, set a deadline. Do everything you can to finish the project by the deadline, but be done with it once you have reached the deadline.

Change Your Schedule to Avoid Chronic Time Wasters

There are chronic time wasters in everybody's life. Freeways are the most common example in many large cities. For example, a twenty-mile drive can take as little as twenty minutes at one time and as long as two hours at another. The solution is simple: change your schedule to avoid the time waster.

Freeways aren't the only chronic time wasters. Other examples include meetings that go nowhere, lunch partners that always have plenty to say about things of interest only to them, and colleagues that want to "chat a while" whenever you see them.

Our list is far from complete, but you get the point. You can save time simply by adjusting your schedule to avoid chronic time wasters.

Keep and Review Idea Files

The best ideas often come at the least opportune time. For example, you might be reading an important report when the idea for an entirely new project strikes you. Or you might be getting ready to close an important sale when the names of several new prospects occur to you.

Normally we would welcome the burst of creative energy that often accompanies a new idea. However, the ideas and energy are a problem when they interfere with the project on which you are working. Worse yet, you may not know what to do with the new ideas. If you don't do something, you may forget them. But acting on them will prevent you from finishing the project at hand.

We address this problem by keeping idea files. An idea file is nothing but a folder headed "Ideas." You may want to use a different title—we can't print some of the titles we've seen—but the important thing is to keep the folder and review its contents periodically.

Whenever we have an idea that we don't want to act on immediately, we write it on a scrap of paper and drop it into the file. Then we check it every week. This procedure has a number of advantages: We seldom have to interrupt the projects we're working on; we have a more or less complete set of action items for moments of boredom; and best of all, our idea file is usually brimming with good ideas for future projects.

OVERCOMING PROCRASTINATION

The "tricks of the trade" described in the last few pages won't solve all the problems caused by interruptions, but they will give you a good start. However, there is one other kind of interruption we need to discuss: procrastination.

Procrastination is a unique sort of problem. At first we didn't know quite how to handle it because it didn't seem to fit with our outline. Then we realized that procrastination is really a form of interruption. When we procrastinate, we are really interrupting ourselves.

Procrastination occurs when people have decided what to do, formed a plan for getting it done and even assigned a high priority to it, but never seem to "get around" to doing it. Deadlines come and go. Priorities are set, adjusted, modified, and forgotten. Plans are made and cancelled. And all the time, something always gets in the way of what is supposed to be done. This is a textbook case of procrastination.

Does that description fit the way you have dealt with any of the things in your life? If you say "yes," you have been "guilty" of procrastination. We put "guilty" in quotation marks because we believe it is too harsh a description. Procrastination is a very natural behavior. We think that everyone has been "guilty" of it at one time or another.

Take a moment to think about some of the times you have procrastinated. If your experiences have been like ours, there is one common feature. You procrastinate when you really don't want to do something. Procrastination is really a way of avoiding something you don't like. Whenever you procrastinate, you know what needs to be done and you know why you should do it. But you just can't force yourself to start.

Procrastination is caused by the fact that you don't want to do something. We believe you can get over the problem by figuring out why you don't want to do the thing and finding a way to get it done in spite of your dislike.

There are probably as many reasons for avoiding an activity as there are people and activities. However, our experience points to four common reasons why people don't want to do things: they dislike the activity intrinsically, they don't know where or how to begin, they don't see an immediate benefit, or they are afraid of failing. The rest of this chapter will look at each of these problems and suggest some solutions.

Doubt and uncertainty are common causes of procrastination. Some people continue to worry even after they have made a decision. Have they considered all of the alternatives? What if something goes wrong? How will other people react? Is now the time to act?

These are important questions and you are wise to consider all of them before making a major decision. However, there are times when we all have to make decisions before all of the information is in. Procrastination becomes a problem when we drag our feet instead of acting.

Nothing can eliminate all of the uncertainty, but there is a new generation of computer programs designed to help you make the best decision possible on the basis of available information. Called decision-support programs, these programs help you review information in a systematic way and make decisions that are consistent with needs, preferences, and expert judgments.

BestChoice3 is our personal favorite in this category. When you need to make a decision, you begin by entering information about the choices you are considering, the criteria you believe are important, and other people ("experts") who should be consulted. *BestChoice3* uses this information to create a model that will guide your decision. The model allows you to assign weights to criteria and experts so you can make some factors more important than others.

Once you have entered all of the options, criteria, and experts, you are guided through a comparison of alternatives in terms of each criterion. When more than one expert is involved, each is presented with a similar set of choices and their preferences are factored into the final equation.

Using paired comparisons is a common procedure but *BestChoice3* employs a built-in formula to reduce the total number of comparisons required. As a result, even complex problems are reduced to manageable proportions.

When you are finished with the comparison process, *BestChoice3* uses its own algorithm to select the best choice. Results include a rank ordered list of solutions and a bar graph showing the relative value of each option. Reports can be displayed on the screen or routed to a printer.

BestChoice3 has more than enough room for the decisions most people are likely to encounter. You can enter as many as 255 options, 56 criteria, and 54 experts.

BestChoice3 runs on IBM PC and fully compatible computers with 256K RAM, and DOS 2.0 or higher. A mouse and printer are recommended options. *BestChoice3* is currently available from Sterling Castle Software; 702 Washington Street; Suite 174; Marina del Rey, California 90202; (213) 306-3020; for $99.

Getting Through Activities You Dislike

The simple fact that you dislike an activity may be the leading cause of procrastination. We don't think there is any shame in that. In fact, the world would be a lot less interesting and people would be far less challenging if everyone liked the same things. However, you need to find a way to deal with things that cause you to procrastinate. Here are three tips that may help you.

- Delegate or trade activities you don't like. See if there is someone else who will do it as part of their job or is willing to swap responsibilities with you.

- Invest a limited amount of time in the activity every day. You may not like the task any less, but the fact that you only need to spend twenty minutes a day on it can make it tolerable.

- Build in rewards for yourself. Set some milestones—say 10% complete, 30% complete, and so forth—and reward yourself each time you reach one.

Finding a Starting Point

Some tasks are so large and complex that you just don't know where to begin. Others are new to you, leaving you unsure what to do first. In either case, the fact that you don't know where or how to get started can cause procrastination.

Next time you find yourself stuck because you don't know where to begin, try the following strategy.

Step One: Begin by conducting some research. This doesn't need to be formal research, but you should start by looking for information on the task. Read, talk to others, review records of similar tasks completed in the past, or simply sit down and think things through.

Step Two: Break the project into smaller pieces. See if you can divide the overall project into pieces so small that you can do each of them in a few hours or less.

Step Three: Do a piece at a time. Some projects will break into a logical sequence of activities. Others will break into a bunch of seemingly unrelated tasks. In either case, pick one task and do it as quickly as possible.

Step Four: Review your progress from time to time. This is similar to the project management approach we introduced in chapter 2. Keep track of your progress by comparing the things you have gotten done with your overall plan.

Looking for the Payoff

Many important projects do not have an immediate payoff. This is especially common in business where you may need to work long, hard hours to build a customer base before you get a significant return. It can also be true early in your career while you are "learning the ropes" and hoping to get ahead.

It has been said that bigger payoffs always call for longer lead times. We don't know that that is always true, but we do know that you need to find ways to get things done when there is no immediate benefit. Here are some ideas that may help you.

- Visualize each step in terms of the long range goal or project. Think about the things you are doing as parts of the larger whole and remember what you are building.

- Reward yourself whenever you reach an important milestone. You've worked hard to get this far and deserve a treat.

- Build a support group of friends, family members, or associates who share your hopes and can encourage you along the way. Many professional associations are designed to share ideas and support colleagues, and there are also service clubs that can perform the same function.

Building on Success

"Perfectionism" is another name for fear of failure. No matter what you call it, it turns into procrastination when someone is so concerned about what others will think that they seldom finish the things they start. We aren't sure how common this problem is, but we know it is one of the toughest. It is hard to deal with because fears may be rooted deeply in personality and experience. Extreme cases call for professional assistance, but here are some simple steps you can take for yourself.

- Build confidence by tackling small, less visible projects first. After you build a record of success, you may be ready to move up to larger, more visible projects.

- Concentrate on personal rewards. Work on projects that have private rewards that you can enjoy no matter what anyone else thinks.

- Determine to finish a task by a specific deadline. You want to make the deadline as important as anyone else's reaction.

- Find or build a support group. You are not alone in suffering from perfectionism. The experiences of others may help you cope.

CONCLUSION

This was a fun chapter to write because it touches on so many opportunities. You may not feel comfortable with all of the techniques described, but all of them have worked for someone, someplace.

Here's what we'd like you to do with the ideas from this chapter. Pick three or four and try them for a couple weeks. Make a list of the things you want to try and keep the list where you can refer to it often. Your personal productivity notebook would be a good place.

After a two-week trial, decide which techniques helped and which didn't. Continue using the ones that helped, and pick one or two more to replace the ones that didn't. Continue trying and testing until you have gotten the time wasters in your life under control.

Finally, you may want to share some of your experiences with us. Write to us in care of Addison-Wesley. Let us know what works and what doesn't. And send along your own "tricks of the trade."

SELECTED READINGS

Anonymous. "85 Terrific Tips from our Busy, Busy Editors." *McCalls*, January 1985, 117–21.

Anonymous. "The ABCs of Time Management." *Managers Magazine*, September 1988, 27.

Barkas, Jan L. "How To Stop Postponing Your Life; Here Are 20 Valuable Time-Management Strategies That Can Help You Accomplish More With Less Stress and Pressure." *Working Woman*, May 1985, 31–32.

Blanchard, Kenneth H., William Oncken, and Hal Burrows. *The One Minute Manager Meets the Monkey.* New York: William Morrow and Co., 1989.

Bliss, Edwin C. *Doing It Now.* New York: Charles Scribner's Sons, 1983.

Blishak, Sylvia. "Turn Away Time Wasters." *Nation's Business*, March 1988, 69.

Burka, Jane B., and Lenora M. Yuen. *Procrastination.* Reading, Massachusetts: Addison-Wesley Publishing Company, 1983.

Douglass, Merrill E. "Do You Have To Suffer From All Those Interruptions?" *Management Solutions*, July 1987, 40–43.

Eisenberg, Ronni, with Kate Kelly. *Organize Yourself.* New York: Macmillan Publishing Company, 1986.

Fanning, Tony, and Robbie Fanning. *Get It All Done and Still Be Human.* Rev. ed. Menlo Park, California: Kali House, 1990.

Godner, Janet. "33 Great Ways to Simplify Your Life." *Changing Times*, June 1989, 22–28.

Grove, Andrew S. "How To Get More Done In Fewer Hours," *Working Woman*, July 1989, 20–22.

Hemphill, Barbara. "Time Management: Control the Paper Flow." *Executive*, Spring 1985, 36–38.

Hobbs, Charles. *Time Power.* New York: Harper & Row, Publishers, Inc., 1987.

Levinson, Harry, and John Elder. "Always Swamped? It's Your Problem, You Can Solve It." *Working Woman*, September 1986, 27–28.

Moskal, Brian S. "No Interruptions, Please!" *Industry Week*, 13 October 1986.

Nelton, Sharon. "Getting It All Done." *Working Woman*, December 1985, 92–96.

Oseland, Malanie, and Brian H. Kleiner. "Slamming the Door on Interruptions." *Management World*, January-February 1988, 37–38.

Pell, Arthur R. "Plagues That Steal Your Time" *Managers Magazine*, November 1988, 25–26.

Schlenger, Sunny, and Roberta Roesch. *How to be Organized in Spite of Yourself.* New York: New American Library, 1989.

Chapter 4

MANAGING OTHERS' TIME

DELEGATION AT HOME
AND AT WORK

You can't imagine how excited I was when I got my first assistant. That was a big step for me and I thought things were going to be wonderful. "At last," I thought, "there is someone to do the routine things while I concentrate on the stuff that really matters."

That was a wonderful thought but it didn't take long to go sour. In just two weeks I realized that we weren't getting anything done: my assistant didn't know how to do most of the stuff he was supposed to do, and showing him how took twice as much time as doing it myself.

I learned a lot from that experience. First, I learned to be more careful when I hire somebody. Second, and probably most important, I've learned that other people can eat up too much time if you don't watch out.

This manager's sentiments are typical of those who have been "burned" by people that were supposed to work for or with them. Almost everyone looks forward to working with other people, and almost everyone soon realizes that having another person around doesn't necessarily mean you get more done in less time.

The important point is that managing other people's time takes special skills. To understand the need for those skills, we need to look at both the promises and the realities of management.

THE PROMISES OF MANAGEMENT

Working with other people is one of the rewards of most jobs. Sometimes "working with" means sharing tasks and responsibilities with peers or colleagues. Sometimes it means delegating work to subordinates and keeping an eye on their work. And sometimes it means doing your part of a large project while coordinating your work with that of others.

No matter what "working with" means to you, you have probably made some assumptions about what it should be like. These assumptions are what we call the promises of management. Let's look at some of the more common promises.

First, many people think working with means sharing tasks or responsibilities. They think that each person will do his or her share so that they can get far more done working together than they could if each worked alone.

Second, many people think about a sensible "division of labor." This is a traditional way of thinking about work in organizations. The big advantage is that each person does what he or she does best. Each knows and does a particular job better than anyone else. As a result, work flows smoothly throughout the organization.

Third, working with other people is often an opportunity to learn. In fact, apprenticeships were the only way to learn crafts in primitive societies. Mentoring programs in modern organizations are designed to achieve the same objectives.

Fourth, working with other people often provides a back-up or fail-safe mechanism. If one person is absent or can't do part of the job, someone else can step in.

Fifth, working with other people may help everyone be more creative. "Two heads are better than one" is a common saying. Recent research has shown it to be true, at least under the proper circumstances.

Sixth, two people working together may have more contacts or resources than any one individual. By combining their resources, coworkers can do far more together than any of them could individually.

Finally, working with other people provides social and emotional support. Researchers say everyone needs some human contact. Relationships on the job are as important as any other relationships. In addition, when organizations undergo massive transitions coworkers can often provide more assistance than even trained counselors.

That is an impressive set of promises. It's no wonder that people often look forward to working with others. Unfortunately, the promises often give way to anger and frustration. These emotions result from what cynics call the realities of management.

THE REALITIES OF MANAGEMENT

Almost all of us have had the experience of working with someone who disappointed us. This disappointment is particularly acute for managers relying on employees who lack the caring, dedication, and/or skills needed to get the job done. These are the employees who "take more than they give," "eat up your time," and "cause nothing but problems."

Almost every manager can list problems caused by these employees. The three we see most often are missed deadlines, sloppy or incomplete work, and irresponsibility. Let's take a brief look at each.

Missed deadlines are many managers' biggest headaches. Whereas employees may see only isolated tasks, managers see the larger whole. Missed deadlines on even a small part can delay an entire project. In turn, a delayed project can jeopardize the whole organization. Getting back on schedule calls for long hours, increased costs, and personal and professional frustration. Failure to get back on schedule may even threaten the manager's career.

Sloppy or incomplete work also costs time and money. Both are required to correct the problems. Worse yet, some problems may never be corrected. Angry customers and inconvenienced suppliers may simply decide to do business elsewhere. Even if a manager can smooth things over, critical relationships may never recover.

Finally, irresponsible employees can do irreparable damage. They may expose the organization to unacceptable risks when they make the wrong decisions. At the same time, they may create needless bottlenecks when they choose not to make decisions. And no matter what the outcome, just keeping an eye on an irresponsible employee can consume hours and hours of the manager's time.

Any one of these problems can turn managerial work into a nightmare. What makes the difference between the promises and the realities of management? Read on!

LIVING WITH THE REALITIES

Several things may explain the difference between the promises and realities of management. Angry managers point to lazy, uncaring, and unskilled employees. Curiously, these employees often think they are doing exactly what the manager expects. When problems erupt, they don't understand their managers' reactions and they explain problems away by pointing to personal difficulties, financial pressures, or other factors.

Searching for explanations isn't always bad—it often helps to understand your coworkers. But the search may not highlight the real issues. Moreover, explanation is not action and things may continue to get worse until someone acts. In most organizations, it's the manager who is expected to act.

We've taken a pretty strong position and some of our seminar participants object. "We're not baby sitters," they say. "We shouldn't have to hold our employees' hands all day." We agree! But action is needed and managers are usually in the best position to do something. Coaching and delegation are good places to start.

COACHING AND DELEGATION

Coaching and delegation are companion processes. They go hand in hand, and it is difficult to talk about one without considering the other. However, it often helps to talk about them as if they were separate processes.

In the most general terms, delegation is the process of assigning work to subordinates. Coaching is the process of helping subordinates develop or polish their skills.

We're interested in coaching and delegation here because they are at the core of every manager's job. Do them well, and the people around you will grow and develop while you have increasing mastery of your own time. Do them poorly and you will see your time consumed in needless frustration.

Of course, both coaching and delegation take time. But the amount of time required by each act of delegation will go down when you work with someone over a period of time. This is true because you come to understand one another almost intuitively after a while. But no matter how long you work with someone, there is still a minimum level of time required to get the job done correctly.

There is another way to look at coaching and delegation. Rather than seeing them as problems, you can accept the fact that they are part and parcel of your job. You could be doing something else with your time, something "important," but there are few things that offer greater rewards than developing subordinates and increasing your organization's ability to get things done.

This second perspective is important because it will also help you avoid needless frustration. Whatever else you would like to be doing, coaching and delegation are essential parts of any manager's job. You might as well accept that and do them as effectively and efficiently as possible.

In this chapter, we will talk about the delegation process first. Then we will introduce some coaching strategies that can help to control the problems caused by missed deadlines, sloppy or incomplete work, and irresponsibility. Finally, we'll talk about the ways these strategies can be used at home and elsewhere.

THE DELEGATION PROCESS

By itself, delegation sounds like it ought to be pretty simple. In our seminars, some experienced managers complain about making it such a "big deal." "Why worry about it?" they ask. "You just tell someone what to do and keep after them until they do it!"

The problem is that "keeping after them" often takes more time than doing the job yourself. We believe there is a better way, a way that will help you to make more effective use of your time as a manager.

We begin by saying that delegation is actually a relatively complex process composed of four steps. Each step is important: skipping any of them can lead to problems down the line.

Selecting a capable subordinate is the first step. By "capable," we mean a subordinate who has the needed skills and attributes or who can develop them in time to get the job done. This can be a problem when you don't have anyone who is just right for the job. You may be forced to choose between subordinates who are not quite ready and those who could do the job with their eyes closed. If this happens often, you probably need to take a good look at your organization's hiring and training policies. However, getting through the immediate problem is our concern here.

When you find yourself choosing between subordinates who are not quite ready and those who could do the job too easily, we recommend you pick a subordinate who isn't quite ready. Then—and this is absolutely essential—provide needed training and development along the way. We know this is a controversial recommendation, but we think it is the right one because training the subordinate will help you avoid the problem in the future. Moreover, a subordinate who could do the job too easily may be bored and give the task less attention than it deserves.

The second step is explaining the task to the subordinate. The hard part is explaining the job in terms that are meaningful to the subordinate. The key to effective delegation is remembering that each subordinate is a unique individual. Some subordinates need very specific instructions focusing on each task: do this, do that, and so forth. Other subordinates would chafe at such precise directions. "Just tell me what you want and let me figure out how to do it" summarizes their attitude. The majority of people fall somewhere between these two extremes.

Your knowledge and sensitivity can help you find the best way to deal with each person. However you should never assume that someone knows what to do. Guard against uncertainty by asking a question or two. Some managers ask their subordinates to paraphrase directions, but this may offend some subordinates. So we've learned to ask some open-ended questions. The questions we use most often are listed below.

What do you plan to do first?

How do you intend to keep track of your progress?

Who will you ask for help?

When will you get started?

How often will you check with me?

What problems do you anticipate?

Giving the subordinate enough authority to do the job is the third step. This is never easy, especially if you don't really trust the subordinate. Some managers get nervous because they see part of their job slipping away. But slipping away is exactly what you want to happen. The more things that slip away, the more time you will have to concentrate on things that really matter to you.

Other managers get nervous because they know it's still their necks on the block. We understand their concern. The important thing is staying close enough to act if you see something going wrong. This calls for balance because you want to be close without becoming so involved that you get stuck doing the job yourself. Managing the fourth step will help you maintain a good balance.

The final step is making arrangements to keep in touch. Few subordinates know instinctively how often or when to check with you. Asking for help too often makes them look incompetent. Not asking for help often enough is dangerous because they may get into so much trouble that you will never get things sorted out.

The tough thing is that there are no generally accepted definitions of "too often" and "often enough." Again, your judgment and sensitivity is the best guide to deciding how much contact is enough. Young, inexperienced subordinates need more attention than older, seasoned employees. And you will probably want to stay closer to "hot" projects than to routine matters.

While a general "feel" or sense is probably adequate for most purposes, you need to be very clear about three items. First, you need to make sure that the subordinate knows when you expect progress reports. Although it seems extreme, there may be occasions when you want progress reports hourly or daily. In other cases, you may be satisfied with reports on a weekly or monthly basis.

Second, you need to make sure the subordinate understands what kind of reports you expect. Many managers are satisfied with casual reports. For them, "everything is going just fine" would be enough. Other managers expect more detailed reports. Some even expect formal presentations or elaborate written reports. Many managers are satisfied with casual reports some of the time while expecting more formal reports on other occasions. There is no simple right or wrong, but you should make sure your subordinates know exactly what you expect on each project.

Third, you should make sure the subordinate knows when to call for help. Some tasks are so precise that any deviation from the norm is a sign of trouble. Other tasks are loosely defined and subordinates are expected to pick their way through predictable mine fields. We don't know any generally accepted rules. But we do know you should take time to explain the kinds of problems that should be brought to your attention.

As you can see, delegation is a more complex process than many people expect. Doing it right takes more time than simply shouting orders. Fortunately, the payoff is reduced anger and frustration along the way. Use the following check list to help you get used to doing all four steps each time you delegate a task.

DELEGATION CHECKLIST

- Select a capable subordinate

- Provide needed training and support

- Explain the project

- Ask questions to confirm understanding

- Delegate enough authority

- Arrange to keep in contact

- Explain when and how progress reports should be made

- Identify problems that should be brought to your attention

THE LESSONS OF EXPERIENCE

As we said, coaching and delegation are companion processes, and it's hard to separate one from the other. However, most people think about coaching as what you do when there is a problem. After all, the football coach only gets involved when the team screws up. Right? Well, not exactly. The coach does become especially important when something goes wrong. The same is true of the manager. In fact, people use the phrase "managing by exception" to describe managers who become heavily involved when something goes wrong. That's when some managers spring into action. We're not convinced that that is the only time a manager should be seen, but we do know it is an important time.

Over the years we have been privileged to work with many skilled and dedicated managers. We have learned a lot from their experiences and we want to share four key points with you. We think they are even more important than the specific techniques discussed in the next sections.

First, coaching is more than giving pep talks. Building morale is fine, but morale alone won't overcome problems caused by insufficient knowledge or skill. The best coaches, in athletics and elsewhere, always make sure their people have the mental and physical tools needed to do the job. When people lack needed skills and knowledge, coaches become teachers. And teachers approach problems in some special ways. The rules for teaching printed on this page highlight some important features.

RULES FOR TEACHING

1. Almost everyone enjoys learning; few people enjoy being taught.
2. Adults learn best when they are actively involved in the process.
3. Trust and support promote learning; suspicion and criticism create defensiveness.
4. The best teachers see things from the student's point of view.
5. Effective teachers are more than sources of information; they are role models for their students.

Second, it's important to remember that problems won't go away unless you do something. Things seldom get better by themselves and it is futile to hope that some magic will transform your problem employees.

Avoiding a problem can leave you buried under a pile so big that you can never dig yourself out. Worse yet, problems may cascade when other employees see you overlooking problems caused by one of their coworkers. "Why should I knock myself out," they ask, "when someone else gets away with murder?" We think it's a fair question.

The key to getting out of the trap is knowing why managers fail to resolve some problems. More often than not, people avoid problems they don't know how to solve. But as a manager, you can't afford to ignore problems. You have to take the initiative and search for solutions. Begin with friends and colleagues, move on to personnel or human resource specialists, and if necessary bring in a skilled outsider. Recently, many managers have learned to get help from an unexpected source: the employees themselves.

The third thing we'd like you to remember about coaching is that what you do is as important as what you say. To be effective, coaching should be an ongoing process so that employees can learn at a steady pace. Saving criticism for annual appraisals or monthly meetings may seem to make your life easier, but it does little to help subordinates grow. In the long run, "gunny sacking" is self-defeating and only makes your job harder and less pleasant.

Providing feedback is an essential part of the coaching process. You need to make a special effort to get to the employee as soon as possible when the feedback is negative—immediately after an incident is the best time. However, there is an exception. When you are angry, it may be wise to wait until you are in control of your temper. Other than that, sooner is always better than later.

Finally, coaching is effective only when you have your subordinates' attention. The best way to get their attention is to make sure they know you are "minding the store." That usually translates into managing rewards and punishments on a daily basis.

Giving someone a raise in spite of inadequate performance is the surest sign you are not minding the store. Failing to punish someone for repeated violations sends the wrong message to everyone. Conversely, failing to reward someone for consistent effort is a sure way to convince employees that they "can't get ahead here." It's essential to manage the reward system if you want to get and hold your employees' attention.

Managing rewards sounds good, in theory, but what can you do when contracts or other restrictions limit your ability to reward outstanding performers? Get creative. Money isn't the only reward employees value. Other rewards include friendship, attention, a feeling of being "in" on things, and opportunities to do interesting work. As a manager you control all of these, and there is seldom a financial limit on them.

In the following sections, we'll look at some coaching strategies that can be used to overcome common problems caused by missed deadlines, sloppy or incomplete work, and irresponsibility.

PUT AN END TO MISSED DEADLINES

Missed deadlines tops the list of most managers' frustrations. A missed deadline can jeopardize a project, and a troubled project can jeopardize an entire company.

Some managers have encountered employees who never get anything done on time. They compensate by assigning critical tasks to the employees they trust.

We can't fault the logic of this approach. However, some of the consequences are objectionable. It doesn't take long for your employees to figure out what is going on. Those that don't want to contribute soon realize that missing a few deadlines is the best way to get out of work.

Employees with key assignments recognize the pattern as well. They may feel abused and start looking for greener pastures if you aren't careful. Even if no one else figures out what's going on, you still pay the biggest price: things never get any better!

In our seminars, we introduce three tools that work well, even with problem employees. But if the employees still don't learn to meet deadlines, these tools provide the documentation you need to initiate progressive discipline.

Delegation Lists

The first tool is a simple delegation list. Its value is in focusing your attention on deadlines. Your employees will see how serious you are when they notice you follow up on every assignment.

The list doesn't require any specialized form or technology; it's really just an action list for each job or task. For each task, we record the following:

Who is to do the job

When the job is to be completed

When the job was assigned

What the job entails

If you have begun documenting performance problems, you can add dates for progress reports and the date a task is actually completed. Table 4.1 is a sample from one of our seminars. Notice that we've organized this list by due dates. This order makes it easy to begin each day by reviewing jobs that need to be completed. Then we make a mental note to check with the people responsible for each.

You might also arrange your list by the people to whom the job is assigned, as we've done in Table 4.2. This order makes it easy to check with each person. Whenever you see these people, you can quickly run down the list checking on all of their assigned tasks.

Table 4.1 SAMPLE DELEGATION LIST BY DEADLINES

Person	Deadline	Assigned	Task
BobR	28 May	01 May	project management proposal
BobR	12 June	22 May	inventory tracking proposal
KarenP	15 June	15 March	product launch schedule
KarenP	04 July	07 May	billing system proposal
BillJ	15 July	ongoing	quarterly report
KarenP	15 July	ongoing	quarterly report
BobR	15 July	ongoing	quarterly report
SteveS	15 July	ongoing	quarterly report
SteveS	13 August	12 March	Hanson report

Table 4.2 SAMPLE DELEGATION LIST BY PEOPLE

Person	Deadline	Assigned	Task
KarenP	15 June	15 March	product launch schedule
KarenP	04 July	07 May	billing system proposal
KarenP	15 July	ongoing	quarterly report
BobR	28 May	01 May	project management proposal
BobR	12 June	22 May	inventory tracking proposal
BobR	15 July	ongoing	quarterly report
SteveS	15 July	ongoing	quarterly report
SteveS	13 August	12 March	Hanson report
BillJ	15 July	ongoing	quarterly report

There are also times when it makes sense to organize your list by jobs. This order is most useful when each job is part of a larger project and you want to see how all of the pieces fit together.

You can easily keep delegation lists with paper and pencil, but updating and rearranging them can become a nuisance. To avoid wasted effort, we keep our lists on a computer with a popular spreadsheet program. The spreadsheet makes it possible to rearrange lists as needed: we can sort them by task, deadline, and person to whom each task is delegated.

A quick trip to your favorite computer retailer will introduce you to everything from relatively limited spreadsheets costing about $10 to sophisticated products costing several hundred dollars. Our personal favorite is *AsEasyAs*, a powerful yet relatively inexpensive program that includes many of the functions found in far more expensive spreadsheets. *AsEasyAS* runs on IBM and fully compatible computers with at least 348K RAM, DOS 2.0 or higher, and at least one disk drive. *AsEasyAs* is currently available from Trius, Inc.; 231 Sutton St.; Suite 2D-3; Post Office Box 249; North Andover, MA 01945-1639; (508) 794-9377; for $50 plus $5 shipping and handling.

Your delegation list is a powerful tool. It really shows your employees that you are serious about deadlines. When they know you are watching, they will begin doing the same.

10-15 Reports

10-15 Reports are a second tool that can be used to help subordinates meet deadlines. They are remarkably easy to use and we know some managers who say these reports are their single most important management tool.

The name, 10-15, comes from the fact that it should take no more than ten or fifteen minutes to write one. Here's how they work.

Every Friday, have your employees take ten or fifteen minutes to write a report summarizing what they have accomplished for the week. Each report should be only one page long, but it should list the employee's major projects, accomplishments for the week, and things the employee plans to accomplish during the next week. Punch the reports as they come to you and store them in a 3-ring binder with a divider for each employee.

Begin your week by reviewing the most recent report for each subordinate. Keep your eyes open for signs of trouble. Are people working on projects you assigned? Are they setting reasonable objectives? Are they accomplishing things they set out to do? Whenever you spot a problem, call it to the subordinate's attention. If it is a minor problem, simply make a note on the 10-15 report and give the subordinate a photocopy. If the problem is more substantial, arrange a meeting to discuss it.

Like delegation lists, 10-15 reports are designed to help you keep on top of things. They let your subordinates know you are watching their progress. And, in worst cases, the reports provide the written record you may need for stronger measures.

Teaching Project Management Techniques

Project management is a powerful tool for organizing your life. In chapter 2 we introduced it for your personal use; we think it can be equally useful for subordinates. When you teach your subordinates project management, you give them the skills they need and you show them that you are serious about managing time.

Begin by explaining basic project management techniques to the subordinate. You can use the ideas in chapter 2 or, better yet, let the subordinate read the chapter. When the subordinate is comfortable with the basics, work with him or her to develop a comprehensive plan for a current project. You may use a simple form like those displayed in chapter 2 or you may use a more sophisticated form.

The form is less important than the way you use it. Give the subordinate a copy and keep one for yourself. Meet with the subordinate regularly and consistently to review progress. Update both copies and use red markers to highlight potential trouble spots. You should expect real progress each week. When things slow down, you need to identify problems and take corrective actions. Sometimes the subordinate needs additional training or resources. Sometimes they need to manage priorities more closely. Sometimes the expectations were unreasonable. In any case, working together on a weekly basis helps to make sure you identify problems before they become disasters.

Young, inexperienced subordinates may need a great deal of supervision. As they become more skilled, you can reduce the amount of time you spend with them on each project. You might cut back to meetings every other week or once a month. Simultaneously, you can begin to reduce the amount of time in each meeting. Eventually your subordinates may even be able to work on their own. And that's just what you want, isn't it?

MAKING QUALITY COUNT

Sloppy or incomplete work is the second source of frustration. It happens when subordinates complete work on time, but so poorly done that you lose time doing it over.

Of course this problem may be related to the first. Seeing a deadline approach, some subordinates rush to get things done regardless of flaws. When you sense that deadline anxiety is the real problem, use the techniques we described above. When the cause seems to be something else, you may want to use the approaches described in this section.

Review Your Expectations

Begin by discussing your expectations with subordinates. You are training them to recognize the expected level of quality. You may even go to the point of comparing their work with acceptable samples.

Although the need for this kind of training may surprise you, it is supported by research into an interesting phenomenon: experts see things that novices do not. Both may look at the same object, but the expert will see and remember more features. While the novice may form general impressions, the expert will be able to identify more features, describe their relationships, and notice defects that were literally invisible to the novice. Because the novice doesn't know what to look for, it's as if they simply didn't see the things that commanded the expert's attention.

Teaching people to recognize problems is literally teaching them to become experts. You need to help them recognize critical features and relationships, and you need to point out potential flaws.

Assign Responsibility for Quality

As long as subordinates know someone is looking over their shoulder, they don't feel the need to be very careful or precise. "Why should I worry," they ask, "when someone else will catch any defects?"

If you can overcome the attitude implied by this subordinate's question, you can solve the problem of sloppy or incomplete work. Follow the same principle applied by major companies in their total quality management programs: simply assign responsibility for quality to the individual. Check their work occasionally, especially at first, but make sure they know that quality is their responsibility—no one else is going to "cover up" or "make up" for them. You need to create a new mind-set.

This raises a tricky question: do you punish subordinates who make mistakes? The answer is "no," and "yes"—that's what makes the question tricky. Here's how we deal with it.

Before a subordinate is fully trained, punishment doesn't make much sense. However, things change once they are able to catch errors. If they don't catch an error and submit sloppy or incomplete work, they ought to be subject to some form of punishment—mild at first but becoming progressively more severe if the problem continues. That's where we get the phrase "progressive discipline."

However, subordinates who catch their own mistakes should be rewarded, not punished. They're doing what you want them to: inspecting their work with care and attention, and correcting problems before passing things on to you.

Set Goals for Improvement

The third thing you can do is to help subordinates set goals for improvement. Use chapter 1 as a primer or ask subordinates to read the chapter and discuss it with you. Then review their performance and begin setting B.E.S.T. goals for each area of their work.

Your own goal setting experiences will help you work with your subordinates. Sharing your experiences will help subordinates recognize areas where it is important to set goals. These are the critical success factors for their jobs. Your experiences will also help subordinates develop reasonable expectations for themselves.

Although goal setting is a powerful strategy, you should recognize one limit in working with subordinates: they have to own the goals. Remember, that's the E in B.E.S.T.—the goals have to Energize the subordinate. Don't expect much progress if your employees simply go along with goals you set. But to get subordinates to own the goals you must be sensitive to their needs and make sure they see that they will benefit personally from meeting the goals.

Here are four things you should do to get subordinates to own the goals:

- Include your subordinates in the goal setting process by soliciting and using their ideas and suggestions.

- Make the goals meaningful by linking them to meaningful rewards.

- Provide ongoing, objective feedback so subordinates know how they are doing.

- Provide reassurance, support, and needed training.

Negotiate an Improvement Plan

You might not think that working with subordinates calls for negotiation. We know it is an unusual use of the concept, but we can think of one special situation where it is called for.

Some subordinates continue to submit sloppy or incomplete work no matter what you do. Heart-to-heart conversations, training, formal warnings, and even discipline don't seem to affect their behavior. Worse yet, there may be reasons you cannot simply terminate or transfer the employee. That makes things really difficult.

When this happens many managers throw up their hands in disgust, but we think you have an option. If you understand the employees' behavior on their terms, you may be able to find a solution. The fact that they continue to submit sloppy or incomplete work in spite of your efforts says that they have some reason for their behavior. They may be "saving face," asserting their "rights," or simply "getting even." Whatever the reason, you need to search out their motives and find a resolution that makes both of you happy.

Negotiation is the process of reconciling interests in conflict. You should think seriously about using it with difficult subordinates. We don't have space here to detail the negotiation process, but there are several books listed in the Suggested Readings for this chapter that can provide guidance. The computer program introduced on this page can also help you prepare to negotiate with subordinates and others.

Employees and coworkers used to be pretty easy to manage. Whoever had the most authority or seniority decided what to do, and everyone else was expected to go along. Since that time, organizations and attitudes have changed a great deal.

Today many managers lack power to order people around, and they may even depend on people who don't report to them. The change has been so dramatic that managers and other professionals often spend a good deal of time negotiating. They negotiate with their bosses and other executives for resources. They negotiate with subordinates and coworkers to establish schedules and project plans. And they negotiate with suppliers and customers to create long-term relationships.

Unfortunately, few people are skilled negotiators. Worse still, they seldom have time to learn strategies and tactics when they're on the spot. If you are in this fix, you may want to try *Art of Negotiating*, a computer program designed to help you prepare for the whole range of negotiations you might encounter as a manager. Based on the writings of Gerard I. Nierenberg, *Art of Negotiating* helps you refine your own thinking and anticipate approaches other parties might use.

Art of Negotiating is remarkably easy to use. Responding to clearly worded questions, you begin by defining the topic of negotiation. Then you identify your objectives, issues and positions, needs and gambits, climates, and potential strategies. Along the way, you are prompted to think about the other party's view of the same concerns. A separate "idea screen" records ideas and options as they occur to you.

Based on your answers and additional ideas, the program generates a carefully prepared agenda that suggests general approaches and specific actions that may be useful.

Art of Negotiating runs on IBM PCs and fully compatible computers, with at least 256K RAM, two 360K floppy disk drives or one 720K disk drive or a hard disk, and DOS 2.0 or higher. *Art of Negotiating* is currently available from Experience In Software; 2000 Hearst Avenue, Suite 202; Berkeley, CA 94709-2176; (415) 644-0694 or (800) 678-7008; for $195.

CREATING WINNERS

The final headache most managers mention is caused by irresponsible employees. As used here, we have a very special meaning for "irresponsible." We call employees irresponsible when they (1) make and act on decisions they shouldn't, or (2) don't make and act on decisions they should. Both of these patterns cause problems. Employees who make and act on decisions beyond their competence may make critical mistakes. They are dangerous because they can expose an organization to unacceptable risks. At the same time, employees who refuse to make decisions cause bottlenecks throughout an organization. Work doesn't flow smoothly because these employees are always waiting for someone else to make a decision.

Both of these problems burn up managers' time. Fixing errors, pushing things through the system, and simply keeping an eye on irresponsible employees eats up time and effort that would be better used elsewhere.

In our seminars, we use a device called the Job Expectancy Scale to help managers clarify their employees' responsibilities. The following pages introduce the scale and then show how it can be used in coaching and delegation.

The Job Expectancy Scale

The job expectancy scale is designed to give managers and subordinates a convenient way to clarify subordinates' responsibilities for day-to-day decision making.

The amount of responsibility you give to a subordinate depends on two things: how much confidence you have in their abilities, and the importance of the job.

When subordinates are new or inexperienced, it makes sense to keep a pretty close eye on their work. This means asking them to report frequently and assuming responsibility for keeping things moving. As subordinates develop, they should assume more responsibility and they should be expected to report less frequently.

The importance of the task is the second factor to consider. Some tasks are so important that you probably want to keep an eye on them, even when assigned to trusted subordinates. Even though the subordinate is competent, the job may simply be so important that close supervision is needed. Other jobs require less time and attention. Some are so minor that they can be entrusted to even relatively inexperienced subordinates.

Deciding how much responsibility to entrust to each subordinate is one of the most important decisions you make. Give subordinates too little responsibility, and they will stagnate; give them too much responsibility, and failure and frustration may result.

There are six levels of responsibility. Let's start by looking at the highest level and work our way down the scale.

At the sixth level, there are some subordinates that can be trusted to do particular tasks without ever reporting. The easiest example is a senior secretary or assistant. This subordinate may keep track of administrative details without being required to report on their completion. For example, a senior secretary might be responsible for stocking office supplies, updating client records, and preparing monthly invoices. If the manager has enough faith in the secretary, the instruction may be given to "just do it, don't worry about keeping me informed." That arrangement has advantages for both the manager and the secretary. It makes it possible for the manager to concentrate on other matters and it gives the assistant a sense of ownership, encouraging pride and accomplishment.

The fifth level on the job expectancy scale requires almost as much trust. It differs from the highest level in asking the subordinate to report at regularly scheduled intervals. For example, the manager may expect a new assistant to maintain supplies, update client records, and prepare monthly invoices. But the subordinate is required to report at regularly scheduled staff meetings.

Like the highest level, this level shows a great deal of trust in the subordinate. It differs in that the regular reports make it possible for the manager to "step in" when necessary. The manager may intervene if aware of problems that the subordinate has not anticipated—for example, if the manager knows a regular supplier will be closing for an extended period and the assistant has not ordered enough material to keep things running until the supplier reopens.

Periodic reports also make it possible for the manager to do additional training. For example, the assistant may not understand the manager's priorities. If the least important clients were being invoiced first, the manager might step in to explain priorities and reorder the subordinate's work.

The fourth level on the job expectancy scale also gives the subordinate authority to act but requires an immediate report. Managers may assign this level of responsibility to subordinates when they want them to accept responsibility but still feel the need to keep an eye on the process. For example, a manager may expect an assistant to update accounting records but will want to act quickly when mistakes could cause problems for other divisions using the same records. Under these circumstances, it makes sense to give the subordinate full responsibility for the task while requiring an immediate report after all major actions.

The third level on the job expectancy scale requires the subordinate to get specific approval *before* acting. At this level, the subordinate may bring something to the manager's attention and suggest an action, but does nothing until the manager gives the "OK." For example, an assistant may be assigned a number of client records, some of which are particularly sensitive. The assistant may assemble a list of updates for such records, but not enter them without the manager's specific approval. Another example would be an assistant who is responsible for ordering supplies, with a dollar value limit specified by the manager. The assistant may buy whatever he or she thinks is necessary as long as it costs less than $250 per month. Once spending reaches that limit, or if a specific piece of equipment would push spending over the limit, the assistant needs the manager's approval before acting.

The final two levels on the job expectancy scale call for little subordinate initiative. They would normally be used only with subordinates that are very new to the job or with tasks that are extremely sensitive.

At level two, the subordinate asks the manager what to do. Even at this level, the subordinate is expected to recognize the need for action. However, once the subordinate has called a situation to the manager's attention, he or she waits for specific instructions before acting.

Level one is the lowest level of responsibility. At this level, the subordinate isn't even expected to recognize the need for action, but simply waits for the manager to say what to do.

As you can see, levels two and one require relatively little of the subordinate. Nevertheless, they are appropriate starting points. As subordinates grow, they should move up the scale, but levels two and one may still be used for particularly sensitive tasks in which the manager wants to be personally involved.

The six steps of the job expectancy scale are summarized in Table 4.3.

Table 4.3	THE JOB EXPECTANCY SCALE
Highest level	6. act independently, never report
	5. act independently, report routinely
	4. act independently, report immediately
	3. recommend action, do whatever directed
	2. ask what to do
Lowest level	1. wait to be told what to do

Coaching and Delegation with the Job Expectancy Scale

The job expectancy scale makes it possible to characterize subordinates' responsibilities so clearly that they are never "in the dark" about their managers' expectations. More importantly, using the job expectancy scale as part of an ongoing coaching program makes it possible to track each subordinate's progress and to pave the way for the next step.

In most organizations, each subordinate is responsible for several tasks. For example, administrative assistants are frequently responsible for many of the tasks listed in Table 4.4.

Table 4.4   TYPICAL ADMINISTRATIVE ASSISTANT DUTIES
screen incoming calls
produce reports and correspondence
establish and maintain file systems
respond to routine information requests
schedule routine meetings
maintain financial records

During the first week on the job, most assistants would be expected to act at relatively low levels of initiative on all of these tasks. As they become more familiar with the manager's expectations, their level of responsibility should grow. For example, Table 4.5 shows the changing job expectancy levels for an administrative assistant at three points during the first year on the job.

Table 4.5 ADMINISTRATIVE ASSISTANT'S GROWTH

	first week	first month	end of year
screen incoming calls	2	6	6
produce reports and correspondence	4	4	6
establish and maintain file systems	4	5	6
respond to routine information requests	2	3	4
schedule routine meetings	1	5	5
maintain financial records	1	3	5

This pattern is a healthy one because it shows a subordinate growing into the job.

Look again at Table 4.5. By the end of the first year, the subordinate is ready to grow beyond the existing job. This can be accomplished in either of two ways. First, the subordinate can be promoted to a more responsible position—perhaps performing similar duties for a more senior executive. Second, other duties can be added to the list. For example, the subordinate might be asked to supervise a group of junior assistants or to help design a training program. The important point is that he or she should not be allowed to stagnate. Tracking the subordinate's development should be a shared task, and both manager and subordinate should keep a record similar to the one shown above. This makes it possible for both to participate in the subordinate's career planning. It also makes it possible for both to send up red flags when the subordinate stops growing.

CONCLUSION

Finding positive, productive ways to work with others has always been one of the central challenges of management. In this chapter we have looked at coaching and delegation. We have also shown you how to get a handle on some problems by putting an end to missed deadlines, making quality count, and creating winners.

We wouldn't want you to think that these powerful skills can only be used at work. Each of them can be applied to your personal life and to assist friends, family members, professional associates, and social acquaintances.

Using these skills away from work calls for special sensitivity. At work you can usually assume that people will follow your lead: that isn't always the case in other settings. You need to be sure you don't intrude on someone else's turf. However, when someone brings a people problem to you, remember the skills introduced in this chapter. Most can be applied to the people problems we encounter in our daily lives.

SUGGESTED READINGS

Blanchard, Kenneth, and Spencer Johnson. *The One Minute Manager.* New York: William Morrow and Company, Inc., 1982.

Blanchard, Kenneth, and Robert Lorber. *Putting the One Minute Manager to Work.* New York: Berkley Books, 1984.

Blanchard, Kenneth, Patricia Zigarmi, and Drea Zigarmi. *Leadership and the One Minute Manager.* New York: William Morrow and Company, Inc., 1985.

Bradford, David L., and Allan R. Cohen. *Managing For Excellence.* New York: John Wiley & Sons, 1984.

Fournies, Ferdinand F. *Coaching for Improved Work Performance.* Blue Ridge Summit, Pennsylvania: Liberty House, 1978.

Herring, Kevin. "Coaches for the Bottom Line: How To Motivate and Encourage Better Performance?" *Personnel Administrator,* January 1989, 22–23.

Jandt, Fred E. *Win-Win Negotiating.* New York: John Wiley & Sons, 1985.

McConkey, Dale D. *No-Nonsense Delegation.* Rev. ed. New York: AMACOM, 1986.

Mayo, Edward J., and Lance P. Jarvis. "Delegation 101: Lessons from the White House," *Business Horizons* 31 (September- October, 1988): 2–12.

Nierenberg, Gerard I. *The Complete Negotiator.* New York: Nierenberg & Zeif Publishers, 1986.

Odiorne, George S. *How Managers Make Things Happen.* 2nd ed. Englewood Cliffs, New Jersey: Prentice-Hall, Inc., 1982.

Onken, W. Jr., and D. L. Wass, "Management Time: Who's Got the Monkey?" *Harvard Business Review* (November-December 1974): 75–80.

Oncken, William Jr. "Get Those Monkeys Off Your Back; Or, What To Do When You're Always Running Out of Time While Your Subordinates Are Running Out of Work." *Working Women,* April 1985, 116–119.

Skopec, Eric W. *Communicate for Success.* Reading, Massachusetts: Addison-Wesley Publishing Company, Inc., 1990.

Chapter 5

BEYOND THE BULL

PRODUCTIVE MEETINGS
AT WORK AND ELSEWHERE

"This meeting will continue until we find out why no one is getting anything done."

This manager's ironic challenge typifies many people's feelings about meetings. For some managers, it sums up what they have felt for a long time. For other managers, it represents a new awareness. Carol is a good example of someone who has just realized how time consuming meetings can be.

CAROL'S INSIGHT

Carol is a forty-five-year-old businesswoman. Many people call her "successful." We agree. While working as a project manager for a large financial institution, Carol has managed to raise two healthy teenagers and has maintained a loving relationship with her husband of twenty years. He has a solid career, but still finds time to do household tasks and he has always set aside Saturdays and Sundays to spend with his family.

Carol's life sounds ideal, but she has experienced growing frustration about one element of her professional career. Her job ought to be stimulating and creative. According to her formal job description, she is supposed to "look into the future" and form preliminary plans to manage the bank well into the 21st century. Carol likes the research she is doing, and she is excited by the prospect of guiding the bank into the future. Unfortunately, there is little relationship between what she is supposed to do and the way she actually spends her time.

During one of our Personal Productivity workshops, Carol discovered that she spends most of her time reacting to immediate problems—"putting out fires and racing from meeting to meeting," as she put it. Reflecting on the situation, Carol discovered that meetings were really a double problem.

First, Carol found that during an average day she spent at least six hours in meetings. These gatherings took up most of her working time, and she hadn't even included such items as "power lunches." Carol had called some of these meetings, but many were called by her coworkers. Some meetings were fruitful, but many were boring, frustrating, and unproductive.

The second problem didn't show up until Carol reread her notes. It was obvious once she realized that she was spending two-thirds of her time in meetings: Carol had no time left for other aspects of her job. As a result, she often seemed unprepared and the meetings took far longer than they should. Worse still, crisis followed crisis because she never had time to "get ahead of the game." And Carol's family life was beginning to suffer because she often had to take work home just to keep her head above water.

MEETINGS, MEETINGS, MEETINGS

Carol's meeting problems are more extreme than those encountered by some other managers, but the problems are pretty common. Participants in our seminars have given new meaning to the phrase "terrible twos." They say there are "too many meetings, they take too much time, and they accomplish too little."

Recent studies show that many complaints are justified. Estimates place the number of meetings in the United States at over fifteen million every working day. Senior executives spend as much as 80 percent of their time in meetings. Companies spend as much as 40 percent of their personnel budgets on meetings. Worse yet, it is often difficult to point to anything specific accomplished by these meetings.

Although it's fashionable to complain about meetings, there is no sign that their numbers will decrease. Why? Because meetings are vital elements of any business. Consider the reasons for calling meetings.

WHY MEET?

Meetings are important parts of any business. Although we sometimes forget why they are called, meetings *can* be very effective forms of communication. We emphasize "can" because we have all seen pointless meetings that drag on and on.

Just about everyone has his or her favorite bad meeting anecdote. But if you look just under the surface of the stories, you can usually recognize legitimate reasons for conducting meetings.

First, meetings can be a very effective means of sharing information. If all of the key players attend, you can distribute information to everyone at once. This saves going back through the "same old stuff" for a number of people one at a time. Moreover, if you overlook anything, there is a good chance that someone in the group will remind you.

Second, meetings are used to create a sense of teamwork. Not only do you have all of the pieces in one place, you can also find out how they best fit together. You can assess how to organize the information, what tasks must be accomplished to achieve future goals, which personalities work best together, and which ones don't. It is an opportunity to build rapport among the people who must work together. This is essentially a social function, but that doesn't mean that it's a waste of time. It's very important for people who work together to get to know each other first. That way we can work to each other's strengths, and avoid stepping on toes.

Third, meetings can be very effective means of developing solutions to certain problems. Common sense says that the whole is greater than the sum of the parts, and research shows that this is often true in meetings. People in meetings can consider more alternatives and give them a better hearing than people acting alone. As a result, meetings are ideal places for developing and testing solutions.

Even when people in a meeting aren't able to come up with a solution, they can often clarify questions. One meeting may "get the ball rolling," while solutions appear at the next.

Developing solutions and making decisions are both very important functions of meetings, and we will have more to say about them shortly. But before we move on, we have to alert you to one danger. Everything we say about developing solutions and making decisions in meetings only applies to meetings that are conducted in an open, participative way. Pressure to get things done, cut off opposing points of view, or limit discussion can interfere with all elements of the discussion process. Poorly conducted meetings may not be the decision making activities they appear to be. More often than not, such meetings simply rubber stamp decisions that have already been made in private. The phrase "group think" is used to refer to this kind of rubber stamp meeting. You should always be on guard against it.

The final legitimate reason for having a meeting is to make a decision. This is closely related to the last reason. You already know that meetings can assemble and process more information than individuals; when everything is done right, participants in a meeting can make a better decision than the participants acting alone.

There is one more thing to think about when you are making decisions in a group. Sharing the process with the people who are affected helps to insure a higher level of commitment. People almost always feel a greater willingness to support a decision and make it work when they have participated in the process.

Put these two features together—higher quality and greater commitment—and you can see why meetings are so often used to make decisions.

PARTICIPATIVE MANAGEMENT

While we are discussing meetings we should also comment on participative management. Participative management is probably the single hottest topic in management today. It isn't hard to see why meetings are the heart and soul of participative management. Meetings make it possible for group members to work together. Participants share information, develop team spirit, develop solutions, and make decisions together in meetings. As a result, the quality of the meetings often determines whether or not participative management will be successful in a given organization. When the meetings are well conducted, there is a good chance that participative management programs will be successful. Sloppy, ineffective meetings are one of the first signs that a participative management program will fail.

SO, WHAT NOW?

As you can see, there are some pretty good reasons for conducting meetings. And meetings are even more important when they are coupled with participative management systems. But what can we do about the fact that so many meetings are boring and unproductive, topping many people's lists of time wasters?

It might be fun to dream about a work place without meetings, but that just isn't in the cards. Instead, we need to find ways to make meetings more satisfying, productive, and efficient. This chapter will share some of the tricks we've learned from experience, both ours and that of others. We'll begin by showing you how to improve the meetings you conduct. Then we'll share some "secrets of survival" you can use when someone else is in charge. Finally, we'll show some ways to use these professional secrets in less formal gatherings at home and elsewhere.

WHEN YOU'RE RUNNING THE SHOW

Many people are surprised to learn that most of the work involved in chairing a meeting takes place before and after the meeting. In fact, our rule of thumb is that you should spend at least as much time getting ready for a meeting as you do in conducting and following up after it. As a result, we'll discuss in turn things you should do before, during, and after the meeting. But first we want to make sure you understand your role as the chairperson.

Role of the Chairperson

We wanted to start by talking about the role of the chairperson because we have seen so many well meaning people get in trouble the first time they "run" a meeting. Many of their difficulties are understandable. Think about things from their point of view.

They have worked long and hard to "get on top." Being asked to chair the meeting is a sure sign that they have "arrived." As a result, they want to make sure everything goes well and they start by showing everyone that they are *in charge*. It doesn't take long for members of the group to remind them of their place, but the process can take needless time and cause needless hard feelings.

We think it's easier to start with a clear idea of the chair's role. We like to think of the chair as a servant of the group. It is the chair's job to make sure that the group has everything they need to make the best possible decision. Getting a meeting space, notifying participants, preparing an agenda, guiding—not directing—discussion, and following up on action items are all examples of things the chair may be called upon to do. Occasionally groups will need some careful guidance to keep on track, but the heavier the chair's hand, the less productive the group is likely to be in the long run.

Now, let's take a look at some of the things the chair should do before, during, and after a meeting.

Before a Meeting

Much of the hard work should be done in advance. You can guide yourself through the process by asking a series of questions: (1) Why are we meeting? (2) Who should attend? (3) When is the best time to schedule the meeting? (4) Where is the best place to meet? (5) How will we spend the time? Let's look at these questions one at a time.

First, why are we meeting? We always start with this question because some long, purposeless meetings could simply be avoided. As you saw above, there are really four reasons to hold a meeting: to share information, to develop a team spirit, to develop solutions, or to make decisions. If you really don't expect to accomplish one or more of these items, you probably shouldn't meet.

Let's look at a typical staff meeting as an example. Most organizations have periodic staff meetings. Many managers say that they have these meetings "just to keep in touch" with their people. We think that is a valid reason; it's part of what we mean by developing a team spirit. You might also expect project updates (sharing information), program reviews (sharing information, developing solutions), and work planning (making decisions) to take place at a staff meeting.

Who should attend? That is the second question. This is a pretty easy question to answer: everyone who belongs to the team, and everyone you would like to add to the team! But there is another consideration: meetings are most effective when there are fewer than ten participants. When you get to twenty or more, about all you can do is share information. With large numbers, it makes sense to have a general information-sharing meeting and then break into smaller groups for building team spirit, developing solutions, and making decisions.

Occasionally you may want to invite "outsiders" to your team meetings. They might include experts with information that will help the team, company officials that team members would like to meet, and other members of the organization who are affected by group decisions. While it is useful to invite these outsiders, we recommend that you do it only occasionally, maybe one meeting in four, because you want to develop the team's identity.

When is the best time to schedule the meeting? This also deserves careful attention. Of course you want to schedule meetings to avoid conflicts with other activities and to insure that most members of the group can attend. In addition, you want to have meetings often enough to preserve a sense of unity but not so often that meetings become boring rituals.

But beyond that, you will have to "play it by ear." Members of the group will tell you when they can attend and they will also tell you when you are meeting too often or not often enough. In practice "playing it by ear" means paying attention to members of the group.

Where is the best place to meet? Think about the possibilities before you answer that question: it has more importance than you might expect. Of course you want to find a convenient meeting place. But there are also advantages in getting away from the job when you want intensive, uninterrupted time. You also need to think about the kinds of facilities and support that are available: meetings that will include lengthy presentations call for one kind of setting, while meetings designed for "hot and heavy" discussion call for a more intimate environment where people can get up and move around. With practice, you will learn to pick the right spot. In the meantime, this is also a good area to "play it by ear."

Finally, how will we spend the time? Remember, meetings are time away from other productive activities: you want to make sure that time spent in the meeting is as productive as it would be if spent elsewhere.

There are few universal rules governing the use of time in meetings. There are simply too many variables from job to job, organization to organization, and person to person. However, there is one rule that almost always applies: develop an agenda before the meeting!

We think an agenda is the single most valuable tool in preparing and managing meetings. Take a look at the sample agenda on this page. It incorporates the tips for composing agendas listed in the sidebar on this page and the next.

TIPS FOR COMPOSING AGENDAS

1. Include only items consistent with the functions of a meeting (sharing information, creating a team, developing solutions, and making decisions).

2. Schedule items so those who are most concerned can be present. In a bind, you may even split a meeting so that some people can leave early or come late.

3. Set reasonable time expectations. A meeting should not run longer than two hours.

4. Schedule items requiring innovation and creativity for the early part of the meeting. The first twenty minutes is likely to be the most creative time.

5. If meetings customarily drag on and on, schedule them immediately before recognized breaks such as lunch or the end of the day.

6. Include all items that will be discussed. "Other business" is asking for trouble because neither you nor the other members can be prepared for discussion of an unexpected item.

7. Solicit topics from participants a week prior to the meeting. You can avoid hidden agendas by making sure everyone's concerns are addressed.

8. Distribute the completed agenda two or three days before the meeting. That gives everyone enough time to prepare but not so much time that the agenda gets lost or misplaced.

9. Include the names of people making reports so concerned participants can discuss matters with them before the meeting.

10. Phrase items in a neutral manner. Never say that the purpose is to "approve" or "reject" an action because you limit the group's flexibility.

11. Include reference to any source materials and reports that participants need to bring with them.

12. Designate the amount of time to be spent on each item.

SAMPLE AGENDA

Department Heads Meeting
January 23, 1989

8:00 Personnel Actions	Karen Howard will summarize personnel actions taken during the last quarter. Please bring copies of the human resources projections.
8:20 Business Development	Marcia Johnson will summarize recent business development activities. Please bring copies of the latest quarterly financial projections.
8:30 Carson Project Update	Steve Smith will bring us up to date on the Carson Project. He also will request suggestions regarding alternate approaches.
8:40 Conference Report	Mark Palmer will outline major developments from the ALAMP conference he attended last week.

9:00 Adjournment

A complete agenda is a powerful tool for use in guiding discussion. Nevertheless, you should also realize that it is intended to be a guide, not a straightjacket. In the next section, we'll discuss some cases where you may want to depart from the agenda.

During a Meeting

The work you have done in preparation will make it much easier to conduct an orderly, productive meeting. Because you have done your homework, you can expect participants to come prepared and ready to get down to the business at hand. We offer the following tips for conducting a meeting. They are really just common sense, but we think they are worth repeating.

- Begin on time. There is seldom a good reason to delay a meeting; waiting for latecomers will only make matters worse. If you aren't careful, the message will get around that you "never start on time," and no one will show up on time.

- Welcome everyone. Introduce new members and visitors.

- Use the terminology of the participants. Be careful to avoid words and phrases with a specialized meaning that may be unfamiliar to the participants.

- Stick with the agenda. You may need to spend more or less time on particular items than you anticipated, but let the group as a whole make that decision. There may be very good reasons for changing the schedule, but that needs to be the decision of the group as a whole, not one or two people.

- Encourage everyone to participate. Don't let one or two people hog the floor.

- Listen carefully and take notes as needed. You need to keep track of the process, and notes will help you spot problems other participants may miss.

- Use a chalkboard or flip chart to focus discussion. By recording comments and ideas, you give everyone a common center of attention.

- Bring the meeting to an orderly close. When time has expired, thank the participants, remind them when the next meeting will be held, summarize action steps and identify people responsible for each of them, and get back to your other tasks.

Following a Meeting

There are a few things you need to do following every meeting.

Make sure all participants receive a summary of the business conducted. You may use formal minutes, but you can often use a simple memo summarizing agreements. Also, be sure to update any project plans or other records affected by actions at the meeting. Explain the group's actions to other interested parties, when appropriate, and be sure to follow through on any commitment you made. Finally, make sure everyone knows when the next meeting will be held and what kinds of business will be transacted.

WHEN SOMEONE ELSE IS IN CHARGE

Meetings are often just as frustrating for participants as they are for the chair. They may even be worse, because most of us attend four or five meetings for every one we chair.

Being a participant may seem less demanding and but it is often more difficult than chairing a meeting. It is less demanding because you are unlikely to be in the spotlight and can "coast" if you haven't had a chance to prepare. But it is more difficult because you have less power to control or direct other participants. We think being a good participant is just as important as being a good leader. Here are some things we would like you to remember about the role of a participant, and some things we think you should do before, during, and after a meeting.

Role of a Participant

A participant's role may not be as difficult as the chair's role, but participants may be more important. For one thing, there are usually five, six, seven, or more participants and only one chair. In fact, there may be some truth in the popular cartoon that shows one business executive turning to another and saying "leadership isn't our problem, we've got lots of that. What we really need is some followership."

The point is, participants can make meetings profitable and productive even when the chair is not up to speed. Conversely, participants can make it impossible for even the most skilled chair to conduct an orderly, productive meeting. That's an awful lot of power: we think you should use it wisely.

If there is one overarching rule for participants, it is to remember the interests of the group as a whole. Meetings collapse, groups disintegrate, and egos are bruised when personal interests and concerns blind individuals to common interests and concerns. You can point the way for the group as a whole if you approach every meeting as an opportunity to satisfy everyone's needs. It may take your colleagues a while to catch on, but you can expect most people to join you if you are sincere and consistent.

Before a Meeting

Preparation is as important for participants as it is for the chair. Always begin by finding out why a meeting has been scheduled and what will be discussed. Often the chair makes this easy by distributing an agenda, but it is your responsibility to ask if you don't receive one.

You should also make sure to clear your calendar—physically and mentally. Clear it physically to make sure you can attend the whole meeting. Clear it mentally so you are not concentrating on other issues or concerns. Your full attention is more valuable than half-hearted participation, and both you and the group will benefit if you are able to concentrate on the issues at hand.

Once you know what will be discussed, there is a great deal you can do to prepare. Assemble and read any background material you need. Begin to develop and test ideas that will help the group solve problems and make decisions. Carefully prepare any presentations you are scheduled to make, double checking to see that audiovisual and other equipment you will need has been ordered.

Finally, work on your attitude. The meeting may be someone else's show, but you have a stake in it as well. Even when you don't agree with the actions of the group, you have an obligation as a member to participate and be supportive unless the group violates legal or ethical standards.

During a Meeting

Active participation is the key to your responsibilities during a meeting. Two items are common sense: arrive on time, and always bring your calendar or schedule book—always! Countless hours are wasted trying to schedule meetings when people aren't sure what dates are open.

The word "active" also has very special significance in this context. We'd like you to think about three applications.

First, you should be active in presenting your views and ideas. Part of the value of any meeting comes from the exchange of ideas between participants. Your ideas are probably as important as anyone else's, and should not be withheld from the group.

However, presenting your views does not mean "talking at length" and it does not mean "beating them over the head" with your contributions. Some studies have shown that there is at least one person in every group that does 40 percent or more of the talking. A small group can survive a forty-percenter but larger groups cannot. Mind your manners and give everyone an opportunity to participate. When your ideas have been fairly heard and evaluated, leave it at that: don't keep bringing them up again. Once the group has made a decision to move on, respect other members' wishes and turn your attention to new items.

Second, active participation involves working with ideas presented by others. Judicious criticism is important when the group is headed in the wrong direction. You can help any group work through very difficult situations by focusing on the ideas rather than on the people. Working with others' ideas may also involve extending them: adding details or support, developing new applications, or suggesting ways of making them more valuable. And you may be able to suggest compromises or other forms of accommodation that will help other participants reconcile their ideas.

Working with others' ideas also means providing social and emotional support. Your posture, behavior, and eye contact should demonstrate thoughtful attention. Taking notes shows respect—as long as you don't appear to be writing a letter—and your notes will reduce the need to ask simple questions following a presentation.

Finally, active participation involves keeping an eye on the group process. Hard feelings can be created quickly when a group hits a snag. You should be prepared to support the leader or other members. You should also be prepared to help get the group back on track. Here are six approaches that can help a group get moving again.

- Focus on things the group can affect. Needless time and attention can be wasted complaining about or discussing things over which the group has no control. Don't let people waste their energy when you can direct their attention back to matters they can influence.

- Use available facts, even if they are limited. Too often groups fail to make use of available evidence because it has some flaw. Don't simply dismiss information because it is not perfect, use it for what it is worth: statistics that are two years old are better than no statistics, an incomplete survey is better than no survey, and experiences in an incomplete trial are better than no experience at all.

- Remember, a little humor can defuse a lot of tension. We aren't suggesting you turn into a jokester, but there may be times when a little levity will do more than anything else to break the ice and get a group back on track.

- Whenever people are deadlocked over rival approaches to a problem, suggest alternatives. When they can't choose between A and B, lead the search for C, D, E, or F.

- Separate idea generation from idea evaluation. Both are important processes, but people lose the ability to generate innovative solutions when they know every word is being monitored. It is better to withhold criticism until all possibilities have been listed than to evaluate them one at a time as they are suggested.

- Look for different perspectives whenever a group reaches a deadlock. Turn choice evaluations ("Should we do A or B") into problem assessments ("What are we trying to accomplish here"), and problem assessments into choice evaluations. Just by changing the perspective you may suggest alternatives which will satisfy everyone.

Following a Meeting

Finally, your responsibilities following a meeting depend an awful lot on what kind of a meeting was held and what was decided. At the very least, you should compliment the leader and other participants for their contributions. If your compliments are sincere and specific, most people will respond by investing even more of themselves in the next meeting. You should also follow through on any commitments you made and stand ready to help others do the same. And you may begin planning for the next meeting.

There is one more piece of common sense we want to share with you: following any meeting, especially following one where the group encountered difficulties and hard feelings were created, avoid sharing statements and events out of context. Nothing will do more to damage a group than spreading gossip about their problems. When groups make illegal or unethical decisions you may need to inform senior management, but it is never wise to turn these matters into idle conversation.

INFORMAL GATHERINGS: MEETINGS AT HOME AND ELSEWHERE

After Carol noticed that she had too many meetings at work, she realized she didn't have enough of them at home. Perhaps calling them "meetings" is a bit stuffy, but she found that if she didn't schedule time, with two busy teenagers and two busy adults in the house, they hardly ever even ate together. It's interesting how meetings at work are treated as sacred, yet time together at home isn't. Carol decided to call regularly scheduled "meetings" at home as well—personal update meetings. With her husband, she decided to call them "dates," and with the teenagers they were called "team building." At their first meeting she found out that Sarah had a boyfriend.

Although some of the aforementioned rules are too stiff for home gatherings, many of them still apply.

Encourage participation.

Let everyone have a turn.

Speak each other's language.

Exhibit a collaborative attitude.

Invite comments and questions.

If you go in with a problem, take a possible solution, too.

But most of all *listen.*

CONCLUSION

We couldn't make all of Carol's problems go away, but we did help her clean up her meeting problems. She has also helped her colleagues and employees use their meeting time more efficiently. Modeling proper meeting strategy is a wonderful way to teach others how to lead and participate. If you calculate how many people hours are saved, it translates into hard cash. But don't bother trying to calculate this savings. The difference will be obvious—in the form of more productive, more enjoyable meetings.

SELECTED READINGS

Belden, R. Meredith. *Management Teams.* New York: John Wiley & Sons, 1981.

Bell, Arthur H. *Mastering the Meeting Maze.* Reading, Massachusetts: Addison-Wesley Publishing Company, Inc.: 1989.

Bradford, Leland P. *Making Meetings Work.* LaJolla, California: University Associates, 1976.

Doyle, Michael, and David Straus. *How to Make Meetings Work.* New York: Playboy Press, 1979.

Jewel, Linda N., and H. Joseph Reitz. *Group Effectiveness in Organizations.* Glenview, Illinois: Scott, Foresman and Company, 1981.

Lovett, Paul D. "Meetings that Work: Plans Bosses Can Approve." *Harvard Business Review* (November-December 1988): 38–44.

The 3M Meeting Management Team. *How to Run Better Business Meetings.* New York: McGraw-Hill, 1987.

Woodcock, Mike, and Dave Francis. *Organisation* [sic] *Development Through Teambuilding.* New York: John Wiley & Sons, 1981.

Conclusion

TAKING CHARGE
OF YOUR LIFE

Just by reading this book you have already invested some effort toward developing your personal productivity. We hope that you feel you have learned enough to justify the time spent. You now know some powerful techniques to help you keep track of your time, set goals, manage projects, cope with interruptions, manage others' time, and make meetings more productive.

We would like to close by returning to a pair of topics we developed in the Introduction. These two topics provide a foundation for everything else we have said about personal productivity.

First, we argued in the Introduction that life is generally predictable. In effect, wealth and abundance are measures of accomplishment. That's true if you define wealth and abundance solely in material terms, and we think it's true if you define wealth and abundance in broader terms as well. You may include personal and family relationships, social and cultural attainments, and physical, spiritual, or intellectual achievements.

This is an important theme because it helps you see the relationship between the things you get out of life and the way you spend your time. Recall the experiences of Mary, John, and Carl, three clients we described in the Introduction. You may want to pause here and review their stories before going on.

The second point we made in the Introduction is that much of our behavior is regulated by habit. We seldom think about the patterns that govern our daily lives. Day in and day out, we do what we do without questioning our basic rhythms.

Our habits are important because they make it possible for us to go about businesses without second guessing ourselves. However, habits also limit or restrict our choices. Consider a simple example.

Every Wednesday evening, we join friends for dinner at a local restaurant. By itself, this habit is neither good nor bad. We enjoy the ritual and look forward to continuing these Wednesday gatherings. But the point is, by joining friends every Wednesday we have ruled out other possibilities. If our Wednesday evenings were free, we might stroll along the beach, meet potential clients, research another book, or meet new people. The possibilities are almost endless. Some are more attractive than others, but we wouldn't even be aware of them if we didn't question our habit.

USING WHAT YOU HAVE LEARNED

After conducting seminars for several years, we realize that there are several ways you can use the information we have presented.

Some people will walk away feeling a renewed sense of purpose and confidence. At the end of a seminar, they say "I already knew that," or "it's nice to know I'm doing it right!" We appreciate that reaction: we think it's nice to know we're doing it right too.

Other people decide to use selected techniques. They use the contents of this book as a catalogue of ideas from which they pick and choose. "One from column A, one from column B. . . ." You get the idea.

Still other people adopt a more comprehensive approach. They may say "I really need to do something to improve my meetings," or "I can do a better job of managing projects." People who respond this way usually adopt a chapter or two as a guide and follow the step-by-step procedures we've recommended there.

Finally, a few people will look on the book as a blueprint for recreating their personal and/or professional lives. It is as if they say "Gee, I didn't know I could do all of that," and set out to design a whole new life for themselves. They begin thinking about what they could do. Then they question each and every one of the habits that govern their lives.

Take a moment to analyze your reactions. Do you feel that you "already know all that?" Have you found some techniques you want to try? Have you identified approaches you plan to use? Or have you decided to make some major changes in your personal and/or professional life? Your answer to these questions will determine what you should do next.

If you are in the first group, it's time to put this book down and get back to business. Making a list of techniques you want to remember would be a good idea if you are in the second group. Readers in the third group can set this book aside until ready to start the next goal setting session, project planning period, staff review, meeting, or whatever. But, if you're in this group, be sure to reread the appropriate chapter before making your plans.

Finally, if you have decided to make major changes in your personal and/or professional life, this chapter is for you. We have designed it to provide step-by-step guidance for one of the most important projects you can undertake: redesigning your personal and/or professional life.

THE IMPORTANCE OF CHANGE

If you have decided to make some major changes, we salute you. You are entering a period of wonder and excitement. In a way, you are becoming childlike again. Just as every stone, twig, and butterfly is new to an adventurous child, every conversation, meeting, and project can become new to you. We invite you to enjoy the process. You may learn more about yourself and the world around you in the next few months than you have in several years.

As you begin contemplating change, you need to avoid the do-more-faster-better trap. In both our personal and professional lives, we are constantly surprised by the number of people who seem to overlook a basic rule of life. The rule is simple and direct: *if you keep on doing what you have been doing, you will keep on getting what you have been getting.*

We think this rule applies to both personal and professional settings. And we want to make sure you recognize its implications. If you are dissatisfied with any aspect of your life, doing more of the same is unlikely to make you happier. Rather than working harder or longer, you may need to think about doing different things. If you aren't already convinced that change is essential, consider the following cases.

The world around us seems to be full of unhappy, dissatisfied people. Some psychologists and psychiatrists have long lines of people waiting to see them. Given a chance to talk, these people complain bitterly about things the world has done to them. Yet other people, we call them life's winners, describe the same events as opportunities—chances that have been created for them. What accounts for the differences between these two groups? As far as we can tell, the losers resist change and try to stick with their old patterns. The winners welcome change and search for innovative ways to accommodate themselves.

The second case comes from our experiences as consultants. Some managers gripe constantly about difficulties in finding loyal, enthusiastic employees. "People just don't care about their work any more. They have no pride; all they want is money." We're sure you would hear the same arguments if you have spent much time in these organizations. But if you look just across the street, you may find innovative organizations that don't have this problem. Why? Because managers at those organizations have embraced change and made concerted efforts to get rid of dehumanizing practices that create disloyal employees. Sounds simple, doesn't it? It is.

Finally, many manufacturers have spent the last two or three decades bemoaning their fate at the hands of foreign competition. "How can I compete," they ask, "when overseas labor costs only 14 or 15 cents an hour?" That is a tough question, especially if labor cost is all you think about. However, a handful of companies have emerged as world class competitors. They've done it by accepting change and thinking in broader terms. Rather than looking for ways to cut costs, they have begun searching for ways to add value. Using innovative techniques to improve quality, enhance service, and reduce cycle times, they have created products of such outstanding value that their customers are not seduced by competitors' lower prices.

We have chosen these examples to demonstrate the importance of change. Adapting to new conditions is the key to success in each case. Reading these examples and reflecting on your own life you may find yourself boiling over with enthusiasm. If so, don't be embarrassed: most people feel the same way at this point. We don't want to spoil your fun! However, we do want to inject a few words of caution before we take the next step.

SOME WORDS OF CAUTION

The examples above show what can be accomplished through change—dramatic improvements in our personal and professional lives. At the same time, we want you to be aware of potential stumbling blocks. We don't want to dampen your enthusiasm, but we know there are a few obstacles ahead. Knowing that the obstacles are there may help you to avoid them or keep them from weakening your resolve.

First, opening yourself to change involves becoming child-like. By questioning your habits and patterns, you literally recreate the world around you. We have already pointed out the wonder and enthusiasm that accompanies the process of becoming child-like. If you don't remember those feelings, spend some time watching active children explore a new park or play area.

At the same time, you need to remember another feature of childhood. Children make mistakes. You will, too!

Children's mistakes often result in skinned knees, cut fingers, and assorted bumps and bruises. You can expect your share of the same. The difference is that whereas children's bumps and bruises are physical, yours are more likely to be professional, social, or financial.

Trying something new at work may cost you some points with the boss. Adventures in your personal life may damage your image, and your bank balance may suffer as well.

Thinking about costs can make you nervous. If it does, remember the lesson all healthy children know: *when you stop trying, you stop growing.* Just as a child who is afraid of bumps and bruises never learns to climb a tree, an adult who fears professional, social, or financial costs never learns what they can do.

The second caution is a little more specific than the first: it has to do with your relationships with others. People's lives are defined by relationships with other people. "Significant others" in your professional life include managers, clients, colleagues, and employees. "Significant others" in your personal life include friends, family members, and other social contacts. All of these people are important parts of your life. They will notice changes in you, and you should be prepared for their reactions.

Some people are comfortable with you as you are. For them, change is an irritation. They will resist change because they don't want to deal with something new.

Other people will be intimidated by your efforts to change. "What makes him (or her) think he's so special?" they may ask. Beneath the question you can often detect envy or resentment.

Fortunately, there are also numbers of people who will understand and reward your efforts to change. The rewards may be nothing more than a "well done" or "give it time, you're on the right track." Even this reassurance is important, and you should seek out people who will provide the needed support.

As you grow and change, you can expect your relationships with all of these people to change. You will probably become closer to those who provide support and reassurance. Your relationships with others will probably become cooler and more distant. This is part and parcel of the change process. If it worries you, remember this: relationships are like habits; they help us do some things while they make it difficult or impossible for us to do other things. As one relationship becomes less important, other relationships become more important. New worlds open and new opportunities develop with new relationships.

A LOOK AHEAD

Growth and development involve change. In the following pages we present a model explaining the change process and develop applications for your personal and professional lives. We've designed the applications sections to combine tips from earlier chapters into a concrete, "take charge" program for making positive, progressive changes.

THE CHANGE PROCESS

Growth and change are companion processes; you cannot have one without the other. They have been objects of attention for hundreds of years, and modern scholarship has produced several models. Our favorite is reproduced in Figure C.1.

We like this model because it includes essential elements and emphasizes the circularity of the change process. Let's look at each of the elements.

Most people spend much of their life in a state of balance. Psychologists and others use the term "equilibrium" to describe this condition. You don't need to master the term to understand what it means.

When we are in a state of balance, our lives really run themselves. This is "business as usual." We don't need to pay conscious attention because our habits keep us on track and there is little pressure for us to change.

Balance is a peaceful condition. It lasts until something creates pressure for change. Actually, there are two sources of pressure for change.

Sometimes pressure comes from something outside ourselves. External pressure is created when our environment—the world in which we live and work—changes so that our habits no longer get the results we want. If you think back, that is really what happened to American industry over the last two or three

Figure C.1 The Change Process

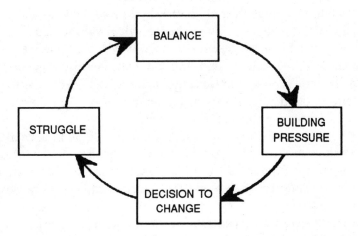

decades. New sources of competition presented so many problems that we could no longer ignore them, especially when company after company began to go downhill.

Sometimes pressure for change comes from something inside ourselves. Internal pressure is created when our wants and needs change. Our habits continue to get us the same results they always have, but for some reason we are no longer satisfied with those results. For example, Abraham Maslow showed that people go through distinct stages in their lives. At times, the need for food, clothing, and shelter is so important that they don't think about anything else. When those needs have been satisfied, people turn their attention to security, membership, esteem, and finally self actualization. Moves from one stage to the next create internal pressure for change. This pressure is just as strong as external pressure. Occasionally, it is even stronger.

You should also note that internal and external pressures may combine. Think about what has happened to cigarette smokers over the last few years. External pressure has been created because it is no longer acceptable to smoke in some places. At the same time, many smokers have decided that they don't want to accept the consequences of smoking. This has created internal pressure. Some smokers have ignored both sources of pressure, but many have chosen to quit.

It is unusual for pressure to be created overnight. In fact, most people ignore pressure for change as long as they can. You can think of this stage as something like an old-fashioned pressure cooker. Pressure builds and builds, even though we may not even be conscious of it. Eventually we have to respond, and that moves us to the third step.

As pressure grows, most people are forced to make a more or less conscious decision. Will they continue their old patterns and accept the results? Or will they change their habits? If they decide to change, what will they do?

These may not be easy questions to answer. Many people resist change; in part, because they like stability and order; in part, because they are not skilled at making changes. If they don't change, there is a good chance that pressure will continue to build until it cannot be ignored. If they do decide to change, they step into a period of turmoil and struggle.

This period of turmoil and struggle is the fourth step in the change process. It isn't always an easy period, and you can often see stress in the faces of people experiencing change. Nothing seems quite right to them. Old habits don't provide reliable guidance, and constant attention is needed to keep from slipping back into old patterns.

Because change requires constant attention, many people give up and slip back into their old habits. Just think about the number of people who have tried to quit smoking and failed. We've seen it time after time, and are willing to bet you have too. Some people make elaborate public declarations and promises. "You can count on me," they say, "I'll never do that again." But within just a few days, they are right back where they started, sometimes even worse.

There is nothing wrong with people who try and fail. Their efforts are the clearest testimony to the difficulty everyone encounters in changing.

But at the same time, there are other people who get through periods of turmoil and stress without slipping back. These people have earned the name "changemasters." Using tactics we'll describe in a moment, these folks make successful transitions. Sometimes they make relatively minor changes in their lives. Sometimes they make dramatic changes—even to the point of creating whole new lives for themselves and those around them.

The last two parts of this chapter introduce an approach used by changemasters. This approach works in both personal and professional settings, and we will look at both applications.

MAKING CHANGE IN YOUR PERSONAL LIFE

Over the years, we have been fortunate to work with a number of changemasters, watching them work through all manner of changes. Our observations are also largely consistent with formal research on change.

Changemasters often have a strong, intuitive understanding of the change process. They overcome resistance to change by using a six-step program that helps them to focus on where they are going and carries them through periods of stress and turmoil. Each of the six steps is important. Skipping any one of them is an invitation to failure.

Step One: Become Aware of Yourself

The first step calls for careful attention to the things that are happening in your own life. Changemasters develop the ability to focus attention of the sources of discomfort and identify specific habits that cause dissatisfaction.

Focusing attention on sources of discomfort is difficult for some people. They prefer to ignore the pressure to change for as long as they can. When they are finally forced to change, they often blunder along without a clear sense of their targets. In contrast, changemasters think about their lives and identify sources of discomfort very precisely. Rather than ignoring pressure for change, they study it. They ask themselves why they feel uncomfortable. They identify internal and external pressures as precisely as they can. And they try to ascertain whether the pressure is something that will pass or something that calls for their attention.

Once they have identified sources of discomfort, changemasters turn attention to their own habits. "What," they ask themselves, "am I doing that causes this problem?" They study their own behavior. They may go so far as to keep a diary recording their behavior and feelings.

Changemasters study their own behavior and feelings because they understand something very fundamental about the world. They know it doesn't do any good to blame problems on outside forces. Instead, they know that each of us has real control of only one thing: ourselves. We might wish the world would change or that people would treat us differently, but wishing and hoping does little good; the world is as it is. We need to change our own behavior if we want to be treated differently.

Step Two: Form a Vision

The second step calls for looking into the future. Changemasters spend a good deal of time dreaming about where they would like to be, next month, next year, five years down the road. Instinctively, they know that you can't make planned changes in your life without deciding where you want to go. Some form images that are complete in every detail. Others form generalized pictures and fill in the details as they go. But both groups have clear ideas of what they are trying to accomplish.

If you have never spent much time daydreaming, now is the time to start. Set some time aside to be by yourself. Think about what you would like to be doing, how you want to spend your time, who you would like to have with you. In effect, create a mental picture of your ideal life.

In addition to daydreaming, do some research. Talk to friends, family members, and professional associates. Search for role models and make a list of people you admire. Observe them, read about them, and look to see what you can copy from their lives.

Conducting research shouldn't be allowed to become an activity trap. Don't let research distract you from your goal, but stick with it long enough to form a clear image of what you want. Once you have formed the image, you are ready to move on to the next step.

Step Three: Create a Plan

Change can be dangerous if you let yourself flounder around. Changemasters reduce stress by forming clear plans that will carry them through periods of turmoil a step at a time. You can copy from them by creating plans with three features.

First, your plans should focus on specific behaviors. Make sure you know exactly what habits you plan to change. If you know what you would like to accomplish but don't know how to do it, you need to conduct some more research. Find out how other people have gotten the results you want, and follow their examples.

Second, identify the order in which you plan to make the changes. Change can be exhausting and you don't want to overwhelm yourself. Think back to the critical success factors we discussed in chapter 2. As you plan to make changes in your life, identify the most critical features and tackle them first. Other things will fall into place along the way if you have focused your attention on the most important factors.

Finally, develop your plan as a series of B.E.S.T. goals: goals that are Believable, Energizing, Specific, and Timed. Write them down, build them into your daily routine, and keep them where you can refer to them at least once a day. Building them into your daily routine is important because it insures that you don't destroy balance in your life. Leave time for personal items so you don't grind yourself down until you can't stick with the program.

Step Four: Act

The first three steps are important, but nothing you do diminishes the importance of action. All of the study, daydreaming, research, and planning accomplish nothing if you don't act.

Changemasters have a few secrets that we all can use. They begin and end each day with a brief review of their goals. They take some constructive action every day. Whether it is large or small, they add the action to their daily to-do list and don't let a single day go by without taking at least one step. Finally, they shift the focus of their attention to concentrate on the change. Other items become less important so they are not trying to do more, but trying to do different.

Step Five: Monitor Progress

Changemasters think of changing habits and patterns as a project just like any other. Using paper and pencil techniques, full scale project managers, or simple ticklers, they keep track of their progress. Day in and day out, they compare how far they have come to their planned time line.

Deadlines have particular significance to changemasters. A missed deadline is a sign of trouble. Changemasters respond by increasing their efforts to get back on track. They may revise their plans from time to time, but they are more likely to change the way they are using their time. Some work longer or harder, but many do not. Instead, they increase the priority assigned to change. Other things fall off their to-do lists until they catch up.

Whereas missed deadlines are signs of trouble, deadlines met on or ahead of schedule are occasions for celebration. Changemasters go to great lengths to reward themselves.

Step Six: Celebrate Victories

Changemasters have one other secret we all should learn: they know that you may never get there if you postpone celebration until you reach the end. Instead, they create lots of opportunities to reward themselves along the way. Each meaningful step completed on schedule is an opportunity to rejoice.

Outsiders may think rewards are frivolous. We disagree because we know that almost everyone appreciates progress. The momentum created by a record of success is hard to beat, and helps to balance the frustrations you may encounter along the way. All major changes are accompanied by frustrations and disappointments. You can't escape the down times so you might as well celebrate the up times.

CREATING CHANGE IN ORGANIZATIONS

Making changes in our personal lives is important and rewarding. Yet few of us are satisfied to make personal changes without sharing the benefits with those around us. Moreover, many of the organizations we value need to change if they are going to survive and prosper.

The changemasters we have studied are also skilled at making changes in organizations. They use the same six-step process outlined above, but they also work on understanding the organization's culture and their role as agents for change.

Understanding the Organization's Culture

Making changes in our personal lives involves identifying habits and developing some alternatives. In organizations, changing one person's habits is seldom enough. Instead, you need to change the collective habits of the people involved.

Researchers use the term "organizational culture" to refer to the collective habits of a group. Just as habits make it possible for individuals to conduct business as usual, culture makes it possible for whole organizations to go about their business. And just as habits produce certain results, so cultures determine how organizations perform.

There is another similarity between habits and cultures: some habits are stronger and harder to change than others. In the same way, some cultures are stronger than others.

We say a culture is strong when it is supported by all or most members of an organization. The stronger the culture is, the more difficult it will be to change. Organizations with weak cultures are easier to change because they seldom achieve a state of balance. Organizations with strong cultures are harder to change because everyone enjoys the equilibrium created. However, the rewards for change are often greater in organizations with strong cultures. This is true because organizations can accomplish so much when everyone pulls together.

Understanding Your Role as a Change Agent

Changemasters working in organizations understand their unique roles. They are leaders and change agents. You may want to ask "What is so special about that? I'm a manager and people do what I tell them. When it's time to change, I tell people to do something different and that's all there is to it."

"Many an institution is very well managed and very poorly led. It may excel in the ability to handle each day all the routine inputs yet may never ask whether the routine should be done at all. All of us find ourselves acting on routine problems because they are the easiest things to handle. We hesitate to get involved too early in the bigger ones—we collude, as it were, in the unconscious conspiracy to immerse us in routine."

Warren Bennis, *Why Leaders Can't Lead.* (San Francisco: Jossey-Bass Publishers, 1989), p. 17.

That brings us to the heart of the matter. No one doubts that you can get a lot done by giving careful instructions and making sure that people follow along. However, there are two problems with that approach to organizational change.

First, there are often times when you don't have authority to give orders. For example, you may need to make changes that affect activities beyond your group or division. You may need to make changes that affect the entire company. Even Presidents and CEOs need support from their Boards of Directors.

Second, even when you have authority, giving orders and following up may get obedience when you really need commitment. Many people will do what they're told, to a point, just because they value their jobs. However they may never provide the wholehearted support that you need to make major changes. We have even seen cases where employees said "Yes sir!" while the boss was around but slipped back into their old ways—or worse—as soon as the boss was out of sight.

Changemasters avoid these problems by becoming models, coaches, and cheerleaders. They model the behaviors they expect from others. They coach others who are learning to develop the appropriate behaviors. And they celebrate the successes of those who work with them.

Being model, coach, and cheerleader all at once isn't an easy task. Fortunately you don't have to do it alone. Building effective participation is the key to leadership, and changemasters use the six-step process we have described to encourage involvement and promote change.

Applying the Six Steps

Meetings are extremely important. In fact, many changemasters say that skillful conduct of meetings is their single greatest asset. Everything we said about meetings in chapter 5 applies here.

Remember that both formal and informal meetings call for planning, agendas, and high levels of participation. You make your greatest contribution by helping people get together, providing necessary information and support, and focusing attention on common tasks. The six-step change process suggests the tasks on which attention should be focused. In this context, the six steps become the game plan for organizational change and the focal point for meetings promoting change.

Sharing information about the organization and its culture is the first step. Although members of an organization participate in its culture, many are so close that they never consciously think about the culture or its effect on the business. It's like that old saying: they can't see the forest for the trees.

Providing reliable, consistent, honest information about the state of the organization is the only dependable way to create awareness. Members of the organization should know how well it is doing, how it stacks up to competitors, whether the trend is favorable or not, and what these numbers mean for them in the future.

Some organizations undergoing major changes bring in consultants to make sure the information is presented in an unbiased manner. Other organizations simply post current performance figures and make senior executives available to discuss them. Both approaches have advantages and disadvantages, but the important point is to make sure members of the organization know how it is performing and what they can expect if there are no dramatic changes.

Forming a vision of the future is the second step. Changemasters approach this step as if they were salesmen. Short "stump speeches" describing the future are powerful tools. Skilled changemasters repeat their presentations whenever they have a chance. It's easy to see why this is necessary.

People need to look forward to a brighter future. That's what they're working for. This is especially true when an organization is in serious trouble. In fact, the more serious the problem, the greater the importance of presenting a bright future. In a sense, the vision is the target at which everyone can aim.

The hard part is making sure people focus on where they are going instead of where they've been. Successful changemasters paint this vision by pointing to examples of successful change elsewhere; within the organization, within similar organizations, even in competitor's organizations. Abstract theories may work in classrooms, but they lack the richness and detail needed to motivate and involve most people. Even small examples can be persuasive, while grand examples rich with detail can form a compelling vision.

The gap between vision and reality is often large. Bridging this gap calls for a concrete plan, a series of steps that logically lead to desired results. Creating a plan is the third step, and successful changemasters display some extraordinary sensitivity here. This sensitivity is required because most changemasters know what needs to be done, but they also know that simply dictating a plan may do more harm than good if other members of the organization feel left out.

Rather than dictating a plan, successful changemasters stand back and let other members create the plan. Sometimes the resulting plan is better than the one they, the changemasters, would have created, sometimes it is not as good. But the important point is that the resulting plan is much more likely to be supported by the people who created it.

Planning must inevitably give way to action. Changemasters do several things to encourage action. They provide support and reinforcement. They secure resources. They make sure the resources get to people who will use them in accord with the plan.

Changemasters also make sure that people aren't punished for making mistakes. They know that it is hard to do new things. Just as children skin their knees occasionally, everyone is likely to make a mistake when they try something new. Changemasters recognize this and they know that punishing people who make errors is sure to halt change. Rather than punishing people who make mistakes, changemasters help people learn from their errors and find better ways to do it next time.

Changemasters also introduce an element of strategy into this step. When the organization as a whole will not support change, changemasters focus on a small piece of the whole. As this part changes, it provides a model for other parts to follow. Changemasters select the part with care, and nurture its growth. Once results begin to show, changemasters display them for all to see.

Monitoring progress is the fifth step. Changemasters make sure the results are presented in clear, unambiguous ways that everyone will understand. They identify relevant performance measures, measure progress as often as possible, and make sure everyone in the organization knows how it is doing. They use bulletin boards, newsletters, executive briefings, breakfast meetings, walks through the plant, and quarterly reviews to spread the word. In best cases, everyone knows how much progress has been made every single day!

Celebrating victories is the final step. Change is hard, and changemasters reward participants whenever and however they can. Financial rewards are often out of the question but there are many substitutes. Public recognition, private praise, and continuous encouragement are often more potent than cash.

Changemasters do one unique thing in this regard. Generations of managers have been trained to look for people doing things wrong. This is what we mean when we talk about "management by exception." Changemasters look for exceptions of another kind. They look for people doing things right. Changemasters know they need heros—people who do things right—and changemasters are always on the lookout for them. Once identified, the hero is celebrated for all to see.

CONCLUSION

This page brings our journey together to a close, at least for now. Please come back and visit us as often as you like. We hope you enjoyed the time we spent together. More importantly, we hope you have benefited from our time together. Now it's time to put what you've learned to work. Just thinking about these ideas won't change a thing. The bottom line is *action*. If you don't do anything we have suggested, then think about the time you have wasted reading this book. In other words, use all of your time either to grow, to change, and to improve, or use it to reflect on how good you feel about your growth and change and improvement.

Time is a funny thing. If you stay healthy, you can tack some time on to the end of your life. You can add more days. But you can't add more time to a day.

A second is a second, a minute is a minute, and an hour is an hour. Time is about the only resource you are given that is finite—that is limited. When it is gone, there is no more. Doesn't it make sense to use it wisely?

SELECTED READINGS

Bennis, Warren. *On Becoming a Leader.* Reading, Massachusetts: Addison-Wesley Publishing Company, Inc., 1989.

Blanchard, Kenneth, Patricia Zigarmi, and Drea Zigarmi. *Leadership and the One Minute Manager.* New York: William Morrow and Company, Inc., 1985.

Bridges, William. *Surviving Corporate Transition.* New York: Doubleday, 1988.

Bridges, Wiliam. *Managing Transitions.* Reading, Massachusetts: Addison-Wesley Publishing Company, Inc., 1991.

Chase, Loriene, and Clifton W. King. *The Human Miracle.* New York: Hawthorn Books, Inc., 1974.

Covey, Stephen R. *The 7 Habits of Highly Effective People.* New York: Simon and Schuster, 1989.

Kanter, Rosabeth Moss. *The Change Masters.* New York: Simon and Schuster, 1983.

Kissler, Gary. *The Change Riders.* Reading, Massachusetts: Addison-Wesley Publishing Company, Inc., 1991.

Kotter, John P., and Leonard A. Schlesinger, "Choosing Strategies for Change," *Harvard Business Review* (March-April, 1979): 109–12.

Langer, Ellen J. *Mindfulness.* Reading, Massachusetts: Addison-Wesley Publishing Company, Inc., 1989.

Nadler, Gerald, and Shozo Hibino. *Breakthrough Thinking.* Rocklin, California: Prima Publishing & Communications, 1990.

Peters, Tom. *Thriving on Chaos.* New York: Alfred A. Knopf, 1988.

Schonberger, Richard J. *World Class Manufacturing.* New York: The Free Press, 1986.

Zaleznik, Abraham. *The Managerial Mystique.* New York: Harper & Row Publishers, 1989.

Index